ST THÉRÈSE IN IRELAND

ST THÉRÈSE IN IRELAND

OFFICIAL DIARY OF THE IRISH VISIT, APRIL–JULY 2001

Audrey Healy and Eugene McCaffrey OCD

COLUMBA

First published in 2001 by

the columba press

55A Spruce Avenue, Stillorgan Industrial Park,
Blackrock, Co Dublin

Designed by Bill Bolger
Main cover photograph by David Stephenson
Printed in Ireland by ColourBooks Ltd, Dublin

ISBN 1 85607 351 3

Acknowledgements
We gratefully acknowledge the following who
gave us permission to use their photographs in
this book: David Stephenson, Garvan Murphy,
Valerie O'Sullivan, Brendan Murphy and *The Irish
News*, *Irish Examiner*, *The Connaught Tribune*,
*Immokilly People, Roscommon Champion, Sligo
Champion*, Pat McCallion, Kyran O'Neill, John
Power, David Farrell, *The Western People*, William
Farrell Photography, Luke Cassidy, Maurice G.
Reid, Ger Lawlor, Jim Campbell, Gerard Hore,
The People (Wexford), *The Echo* (Enniscorthy),
Robert Allen, James Weymes, Ger Lawlor, Pat
Sweeney, Tony Maher, Jerome Rafferty, Michael
McCormack.

Sincere thanks also to the following venues who
generously supplied photographs, though not all
of them could be included: Armagh, Athboy,
Avila, Ballsbridge, Beaumont, Berkeley Road,
Bruckless, Brunswick Street, Bullock Castle,
Carlow, Castlemartyr, Clarendon Street, Clonard,
Cobh, Drogheda, Ennis, Falcarragh, Gorey, Gort
Muire, Kilnacrott, Knights of St Columbanus,
Knocklyon, Limerick, Longford, Loughrea,
Moate, Mountjoy Prison, Mount Merrion,
Mullingar, Newry, Sligo, SMA Cork, Terenure,
Termonbacca, Thurles, Waterford, Adoration
Sisters Wexford, and the Carmels of Delgany,
Firhouse, Glenvale, Hampton, Kilmacud, Knock,
Loughrea, Malahide, New Ross, Roebuck, Tallow.

For Gerard and Larry

Table of Contents

Pilgrimage of Grace

April 15 Sunday *Easter Sunday*
    Arrival Rosslare, 10.30am
    Enniscorthy, St Aidan's Cathedral
April 16 Monday
    Wexford, Bride Street Church
April 17 Tuesday
    New Ross, Carmelite sisters,
    via Cushinstown church
April 18 Wednesday
    Gorey parish church
April 19 Thursday
    Knocktopher, Carmelite church
April 20 Friday
    Kilkenny, St Mary's Cathedral
April 21 Saturday
    Kilmacud, Carmelite sisters
April 22 Sunday
    Beaumont parish, Carmelites
April 23 Monday
    Roebuck, Carmelite sisters
April 24 Tuesday
    Carlow, Cathedral of the Assumption
April 25 Wednesday
    Dublin, St James' Hospital
April 26 Thursday
    Drumcondra, 'Hampton', Carmelite
    sisters
April 27 Friday
    Drumcondra, 'Hampton', Theresian
    Trust
April 28 Saturday
    Ely Place, Knights of St Columbanus,
    Delgany, Carmelite sisters
April 29 Sunday
    Gort Muire, Ballinteer, Carmelites
April 30 Monday
    Dublin, St Mary's Pro-Cathedral
May 1 Tuesday
    Malahide, Carmelite sisters

May 2 Wednesday
    Brunswick Street, Legion of Mary
May 3 Thursday
    Terenure College, Carmelites
May 4 Friday
    Mountjoy Prison and Dóchas Centre
May 5 Saturday
    Knocklyon parish, Carmelites
May 6-7 Sunday-Monday
    'Avila', Donnybrook, Carmelites
May 8-9 Tuesday-Wednesday
    Merrion Road, St Mary's Centre
    Clarendon Street, Carmelites
May 10 Thursday
    Curragh Camp, garrison church
    Kildare, White Abbey, Carmelites (1)
May 11 Friday
    Kildare, White Abbey, Carmelites (2)
May 12 Saturday
    Blackrock, Louis & Zélie Martin Hospice
    Ballsbridge, Poor Clares
May 13 Sunday
    Berkeley Road parish, Carmelites
May 14-15 Monday-Tuesday
    Whitefriar Street, Carmelites
May 16 Wednesday
    Firhouse, Carmelite sisters
May 17 Thursday
    Athboy parish church
    Mullingar, Cathedral of Christ the
    King
May 18 Friday
    Longford, St Mel's Cathedral
May 19 Saturday
    Moate, Carmelites
May 20 Sunday
    Drogheda, Medical Missionaries of
    Mary
May 21 Monday
    Cavan, Cathedral of SS Patrick & Felim
May 22 Tuesday
    Kilnacrott, Holy Trinity Abbey

May 23 Wednesday
Cooley parish church
Newry, SS Patrick & Colman Cathedral
Glenvale, Carmelite sisters

May 24 Thursday
Lurgan, St Peter's, Shankill

May 25 Friday
Armagh, St Patrick's Cathedral

May 26 Saturday
Monaghan, St Macartan's Cathedral

May 27 Sunday *Ascension*
Belfast, St Peter's Cathedral

May 28 Monday
Belfast, Clonard, Redemptorists

May 29 Tuesday
Belfast, Ardoyne, Passionists

May 30 Wednesday
Derry, St Eugene's Cathedral

May 31 Thursday
Termonbacca, Carmelites

June 1 Friday
Letterkenny, Cathedral of St Eunan
and St Columba

June 2 Saturday
Falcarragh parish church

June 3 Sunday *Pentecost Sunday*
Bruckless parish church

June 4 Monday
Sligo, St Mary's Cathedral

June 5 Tuesday
Ballina, St Muredach's Cathedral

June 6 Wednesday
Ballaghaderreen, Cathedral of
the Annunciation

June 7 Thursday
Tuam, Cathedral of the Assumption

June 8 Friday
Knock, Carmelite sisters

June 9-10 Saturday-Sunday
Knock, Our Lady's Shrine

June 11 Monday
Loughrea, Carmelites

June 12 Tuesday
Loughrea, Carmelite sisters

June 13 Wednesday
Loughrea, St Brendan's Cathedral

June 14 Thursday
Spiddal, Cill Éinne Church
Galway, Our Lady Assumed into
Heaven & St Nicholas Cathedral

June 15 Friday
Ennis, Cathedral of SS Peter and Paul

June 16-17 Saturday-Sunday
Tallow, Carmelite sisters

June 18 Monday
Limerick, St John's Cathedral

June 19 Tuesday
Killarney, St Mary's Cathedral

June 20 Wednesday
Cork, Cathedral of St Mary and
St Anne

June 21 Thursday
Cobh, St Colman's Cathedral

June 22 Friday *Sacred Heart*
Castlemartyr, Carmelites

June 23 Saturday
Blackrock, Cork, SMA church

June 24 Sunday
Kinsale, Carmelites

June 25 Monday
Thurles, Cathedral of the Assumption

June 26 Tuesday
Waterford, Holy Trinity Cathedral

June 27 Wednesday
Lough Derg, St Patrick's Purgatory

June 28-30 Thursday-Saturday
From Lough Derg to Wexford Park

July 1 Sunday
Wexford Park, Thanksgiving
Celebration

thérèse in ireland

APRIL 15 – JULY 1
2001

1. Rosslare
2. Enniscorthy
3. Wexford
4. New Ross
5. Gorey
6. Knocktopher
7. Kilkenny
8. Kilmacud
9. Beaumont
10. Roebuck
11. Carlow
12. St James' Hospital
13. Drumcondra
14. Drumcondra
15. Ely Place
16. Delgany
17. Gort Muire
18. St Mary's Pro-Cathedral
19. Malahide
20. Legion of Mary
21. Terenure College
22. Mountjoy Prison
23. Reserved
24. Knocklyon
25. Avila, Donnybrook
26. Clarendon Street
27. Curragh Camp
28. Kildare
29. Blackrock
30. Berkeley Road
31. Whitefriar Street
32. Firhouse
33. Athboy
34. Mullingar
35. Longford
36. Moate
37. Drogheda
38. Cavan
39. Kilnacrott
40. Newry
41. Newry
42. Lurgan
43. Armagh
44. Monaghan
45. Belfast
46. Belfast
47. Belfast
48. Derry
49. Termonbacca
50. Letterkenny
51. Falcarragh
52. Bruckless
53. Sligo
54. Ballina
55. Ballaghaderreen
56. Tuam
57. Knock
58. Knock
59. Loughrea
60. Loughrea
61. Loughrea
62. Galway
63. Ennis
64. Tallow
65. Limerick
66. Killarney
67. Cork
68. Cobh
69. Castlemartyr
70. Cork, SMA
71. Kinsale
72. Thurles
73. Waterford
74. Lough Derg

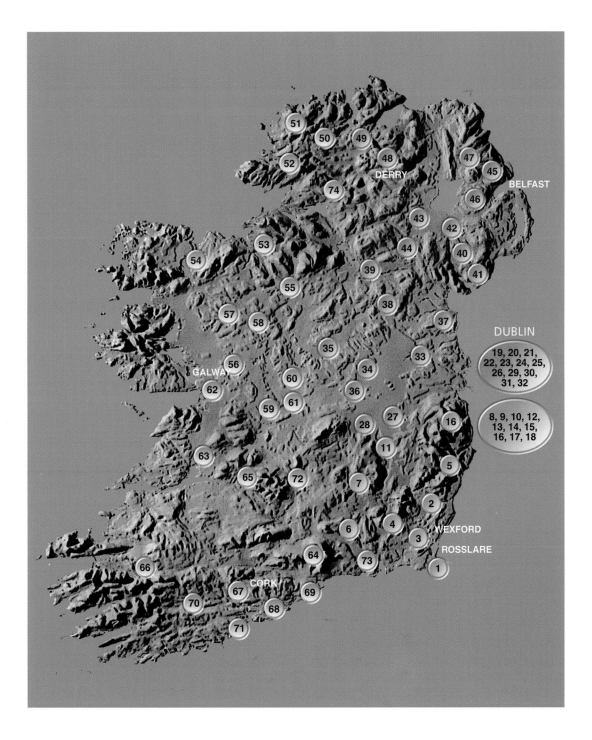

51
50
49
52
74
DERRY
48
47
45
BELFAST
46
43
42
44
40
53
39
41
54
55
38
57
37
58
DUBLIN
35
19, 20, 21,
33
22, 23, 24, 25,
34
26, 29, 30,
56
60
31, 32
GALWAY
36
62
59
61
27
8, 9, 10, 12,
28
16
13, 14, 15,
11
16, 17, 18
63
5
65
72
7
2
6
4
WEXFORD
3
64
ROSSLARE
66
73
1
CORK
67
69
70
68
71

Foreword

In the course of approximately eleven weeks during the summer of 2001, as many as three million Irish people turned out at venues throughout Ireland to venerate the Relics of St Thérèse. To understand what moves Irish people to behave like this, I find the poet, Patrick Kavanagh, most helpful.

> No snow but in their minds
> The fields and road are white
> They may be talking of the turkey markets
> Or foreign politics, but tonight
> Their plain hard country words
> Are Christ's singing birds.
> [*Christmas Eve Remembered*]

The genius of Kavanagh in this and so many of his poems is twofold. Firstly, he is able to look beneath the surface of the most earth-bound things and see in them a world 'charged with the glory of God'. Secondly, he credited the most ordinary of people with the same ability: 'Their thoughts are earthy but their minds move/in dreams of the Blessed Virgin …' The faculty, which allows the human being to see into the inner core of things, is the imagination.

Strangely enough, it is often the most intellectually gifted people who seem 'threatened' by the imagination. Although we might praise people for being 'imaginative', imagination on the whole receives a bad press. Far too often we hear comments such as 'It's all in your imagination' or 'You're only imagining that!'

The imagination is alive and well in children – that is, children of all ages. It takes years of formal education to rid them of this most valuable and creative of gifts! That is why the best commentators on the recent eleven-week visit of the Relics of St Thérèse to Ireland have been the children and the childlike.

Those who commissioned Audrey Healy and Eugene McCaffrey to 'write a story' of the visit were themselves imaginative – and I wasn't one of them! – because it is the story which jumpstarts the imagination, and the imagination, in its turn, fires the heart. 'Poor mind,' as Kavanagh called it, is often left with the rather earthbound and prosaic task of running after its more creative sister and trying to ensure that it doesn't get into too much trouble.

St Thérèse was a great one for the writing. Much of that writing was poetry, a form of literature in which the faculty of the imagination is uppermost. As for story, isn't that the title of her best-known work, *Story of a Soul*?

What an enlightened choice to bring together Audrey Healy, a young woman and a journalist, and Eugene McCaffrey, a Carmelite who has written widely on St Thérèse, to record the story of the visit to Ireland.

Donncha Ó Dúlaing, commenting on the difference between the two great 'visits' of our lifetime – John Paul II in 1979 and St Thérèse in 2001 – remarked that only 'the big shots' got near the Pope, while 'every five-eighths' like myself were VIPs during the visit of St Thérèse.

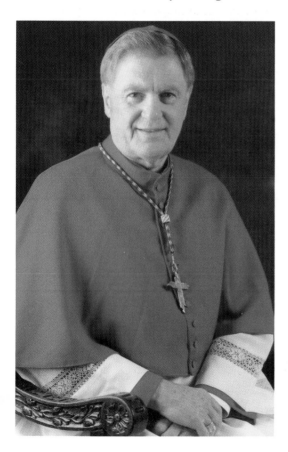

Audrey and Eugene, like Donncha, were 'there' to report from the great majority of the one hundred or so venues in every corner of Ireland. This is their account of what they saw and heard from all kinds of people during those never-to-be-forgotten weeks in the summer of 2001. They have recorded wonderfully well this great event of our times, and of how St Thérèse set the heather and the hearts of Ireland blazing. These days and weeks of grace should not be forgotten. Because of what Audrey and Eugene have written they won't. Thanks be to God.

✠ *Brendan Comiskey*
Bishop of Ferns
15 August, Feast of the Assumption, 2001

Preface

I am very happy that Audrey Healy and Eugene McCaffrey were able to keep a diary of what happened at most of the venues visited by St Thérèse during her Irish tour, 15 April to 1 July, 2001. I am even more happy that by publishing it they will find many people eager to retrace their memories of what has proved to be one of the most extraordinary events in the entire history of the Irish church. It was obvious to all of us involved that St Thérèse, right from the beginning, was working very powerfully in our midst. Much of what happened during those eighty glorious days has been recorded on television, national and local radio, and in the national and local press, but it is important that as much of that material as possible should be gathered into one book, so that not only the many who loved every moment of those Irish Theresian days may savour the whole experience any time they wish, but also that posterity may be able to do the same. The response of the Irish people to St Thérèse even stirred the imagination of the international media – FT1, the premier French television channel, sent a special camera crew to Killarney Cathedral to film the occasion.

When we returned to Lisieux with the Relics on 3 July, the Rector, Père Raymond Zambelli, informed us that the Irish veneration figures (almost 75% of the total population) were the highest of any country to date. *The Sunday Business Post* of 24 June described the whole event as 'the greatest mass movement of Irish people in the history of the country'. A statement like that gives added urgency to this book. So many things happened. So many people got involved. Virtually every group on the local scene offered its services and was anxious to participate. Indeed, many individuals who are normally shy of any group did likewise. It was obvious that St Thérèse was powerfully touching so many hearts. I am glad that Audrey and Eugene have captured so much of what happened on this grace-filled tour and that they have done so while memories of so many precious moments are fresh. Our thanks also to the venue hosts, the bishops and administrators of Ireland's twenty-six diocesan cathedrals, as well as the Carmelite sisters and fathers (OCD and O Carm) without whose precious co-operation the wonderful 'Pilgrimage of Grace' could not have taken place at all.

I feel I should add something special. A very important aspect of the entire tour was, by its very nature, privy to the Thérèsemobile team: Pat Sweeney, Jim Doyle, Liam O'Keeffe

and myself. There were many extraordinary scenes of devotion *en route* between various venues, the sheer extent of which we had not anticipated. Knots of hundreds of people, accompanied by many sick people in wheelchairs or in cars, were encountered on the roadside outside churches, hospitals, schools, or at times at crossroads. We could not and did not pass these good people by. With the help of the public address system on the Thérèsemobile, we were able to lead these fervent people in prayer as they venerated the Relics by the roadside. It struck me more than once that the veneration of Thérèse continued without any break, day or night, through every moment of the Irish tour, because of the unbroken veneration in the open churches and the Thérèsemobile.

May all who read this book be drawn ever more closely to imitate the love and childlike trust and abandonment of St Thérèse.

J. Linus Ryan, O Carm
National Coordinator
St Thérèse Relics Irish Visit

Introduction

For three months we had the privilege of living in the presence of a saint. Every day, thousands of people shared this experience. Wherever we went, across the length and breadth of the country, we heard the same expressions of delight and amazement, from 'incredible, wonderful, and unbelievable' to the response of a younger generation as 'cool, unreal, and fantastic'. 'It's magic to be here,' one teenager said. For us, as part of the St Thérèse team, it was an everyday experience, but one that never paled.

After a few days on the road, we started to keep a diary. Audrey, as a journalist, had been asked to record the historic events of which we were part. Each day she spoke to people, listened to their stories and wrote down their responses and reactions. As we shared our notes with each other and with the group, we realised just how unique our experience was. Between us, we had been present at every venue. Most people could attend only one or, at most, a few locations but were interested to know something of what happened in other parts of the country. Thus, the shape of the book gradually fell into place: a diary of a visit.

We have tried to pick out what was unique to each venue. We could not, of course, hope to capture adequately the experience in each venue: each location would merit its own book. And yet, despite the routine, each day was different and each location had its own spirit and atmosphere. Those who were there will have their own memories and recollections; for others, we hope it will help them to see, in some small way, how the 'Pilgrimage of Grace' invoked so many different responses and expressions of faith.

We would like to thank all who have helped us in the writing of this book, especially Bishop Brendan Comiskey, Fr Linus Ryan and everyone who was part of the St Thérèse team, for their support, interest and encouragement; Seán O Boyle and Bill Bolger, from the Columba Press; Garvan Murphy, the official cameraman of the event, and photographer, David Stephenson, a Thérèse-sent gift who joined us at the start of the tour. Our thanks

also to Teresa Gleeson, Bishop's House, Wexford, for faithfully collating the reports from the various venues, and to Joana Murphy and Joanne Mosley for proof-reading and suggestions regarding the text. Finally, our sincere thanks to each host venue for the welcome and hospitality we received, for photographs and information supplied, and for corrections and amendments made to the text.

Audrey Healy & Eugene McCaffrey

The Organising Committee

VISIT TO IRELAND OF THE RELICS OF ST THÉRÈSE

Chairperson:
Bishop Brendan Comiskey

Coordinators:
J. Linus Ryan, O Carm
Eugene McCaffrey, OCD

Members:
Bridie Ryan
St Thérèse Missionary League
Bernardine Stanley
St Thérèse Prayer Group
Pat Sweeney
Theresian Trust
Noel Smyth
Theresian Trust
Marie O'Grady
Theresian Trust
Martin Ryan
Honorary Secretary
St Thérèse Missionary League

John Keating, O Carm
headed a special Liturgy Committee

The Greatest Saint of Modern Times

St Thérèse of the Child Jesus was born in Alençon in France on 2 January 1873. She was the last of nine children, four of whom had already died. Her father was a watchmaker and her mother ran a small lace-making business. When Thérèse was four, her mother died and the family moved to Lisieux. Here she spent the next ten years of her life, brought up in an atmosphere of love and affection.

From an early age she wanted to give herself to God. She struggled with her own stubbornness of will and suffered a lot from her very sensitive and scrupulous nature. When she was ten years old, she was cured of a mysterious illness through what she described as the 'smile of the Queen of Heaven'.

At the age of fifteen, she entered the Carmelite convent in Lisieux and was given the name, 'Thérèse of the Child Jesus and of the Holy Face'. She spent the next nine years of her life there, faithfully and heroically living the life of a Carmelite nun with great simplicity and humility. She discovered what she called her 'Little Way' – a way of confidence and trust and of total surrender to God's Merciful Love. At the end of her life she realised her mission was about to begin, and she would spend her heaven doing good on earth.

St Thérèse died on 30 September 1897 at the age of twenty-four, after eighteen months of great physical suffering and desolation of spirit. She was canonised in 1925. She has been proclaimed Patroness of France and of the Missions and in 1997 was declared a Doctor of the Church by Pope John Paul II. Pius X called her 'the greatest saint of modern times'.

Before she died, Thérèse, at the request of her sister Pauline, started to put together the recollections and memories of her childhood, along with her reflections on the religious life. Her *Story of a Soul* was published one year after her death. Millions of copies have been sold and it has been translated into over fifty languages.

Her feast-day is celebrated each year on 1 October.

A Pilgrim Saint

I would like to travel over the whole world to preach your Name … to preach the gospel on all five continents.

St Thérèse's wish has been fulfilled. Six years ago the Relics of St Thérèse of Lisieux began a 'Pilgrimage of Grace' that will eventually cover the four corners of the world. She has already travelled thousands of miles from Russia to Brazil, Argentina to Vietnam, USA to Mexico; Africa and Australia are at present preparing for her coming. For two years Ireland had waited its turn; at last that moment had arrived.

The Reliquary containing 'some of the bones' of St Thérèse of Lisieux arrived in Ireland on Easter Sunday, 15 April 2001, and began a nationwide tour that eventually finished eleven weeks later with a Thanksgiving Celebration in Wexford Park on 1 July. The Reliquary visited seventy-five official locations, including every diocesan cathedral, all Carmelite convents and monasteries, and some major shrines, such as Knock and Lough Derg.

At every venue, huge crowds turned out, far exceeding the most optimistic expectations of the Organising Committee. Crowds of twenty to thirty thousand were normal for most venues. It is estimated that over three million people venerated the Relics during the Irish visit. Everywhere there was an outpouring of prayer and devotion. It was a pilgrimage of joy and celebration. Something very special was happening and it was obvious that the visit of the Little Flower had caught the imagination of the Irish people and touched a chord hidden within so many hearts.

Everywhere she went, the same message was proclaimed – the gospel message of love, confidence and invincible hope.

This is the unique genius of St Thérèse of Lisieux. Thanks to her the entire church has found once again the whole simplicity and freshness of the gospel truth, which has its origin and source in the heart of Christ himself.

(John Paul II)

Preparing for the Visit

St Thérèse's gentle humour was proverbial and seemed to be at work when the fax confirming the visit of her Relics to Ireland was received on St Patrick's Day, 1999! The official request had been made a few months previously by the Irish Bishops' Conference. And so, wheels were set in motion and two years of preparatory work got under way.

The first step was to set up an Organising Committee to oversee the preparations. Bishop Brendan Comiskey of Ferns was appointed Chairman, with Fr Linus Ryan, O Carm as National Coordinator, assisted by Fr Eugene McCaffrey, OCD. A Vision Statement was drafted to clarify the purpose and focus of the visit:

> The coming of the Relics of St Thérèse to Ireland will help individuals and groups to grasp the life and teaching of the saint, and to consider and renew their own journey in faith to God.

From the beginning, the visit had both a National and a Carmelite dimension. St Thérèse was coming at the invitation of the Irish church and also to visit her own Carmelite sisters and brothers throughout the country. Thus, the decision was made to bring the Relics to every diocesan cathedral in Ireland and to all Carmelite convents and monasteries. It was then a matter of logistics and endless months of negotiation. Finally, seventy-five venues were selected, spread over an eleven-week period.

The main work from then on was one of keeping in touch with each venue and supplying the relevant information. Brochures were published, background material prepared and communiqués sent regularly to every venue. The Carmelite nuns in Tallow undertook much of the printing work: prayer-leaflets, booklets, brochures and a series of commemorative plates, block mounts, diaries and bookmarks. A Mobile Bookshop was fitted out to travel with the Relics, so as to make available good background literature on St Thérèse. Then in January, a major seminar was held in Dublin for all host venues, and the practical details of the tour were discussed and finalised.

Suddenly, it was all coming together – the joy and anticipation of that Easter Sunday visitor was already in the air.

The Lone Piper

Perhaps, for many, one of the most enduring memories of the visit of St Thérèse's Relics to Ireland will be the haunting tones of the lone piper who accompanied the Reliquary into most churches. The Thérèsemobile was usually met at the outskirts of the town by a colour party and led in procession through the streets, flanked by local groups, hosts of school children scattering flowers, and the music of marching bands. The Reliquary was received with a short Prayer Service at the door of the church and carried shoulder-high into the sanctuary by volunteers, members of the FCA, Order of Malta or other local groups. It was always a moment of special solemnity and never failed to evoke the most poignant awareness that here indeed we were in the presence of a saint.

The Reception Liturgy was deliberately short: a word of welcome, a hymn in honour of the saint and prayers of intercession, often read by children. The service always included the reading of St Paul's 'hymn of love', the famous passage from the *First Epistle to the Corinthians*, which opened up for St Thérèse the whole mystery of her vocation as 'love in the heart of the church'. Read in her presence, the words seemed to echo throughout the church and never failed to touch the hearts of the hushed congregation.

The whole focus of the veneration was Thérèse herself, physically and spiritually present in the Reliquary. People wanted to touch the casket and feel close to her, whisper a prayer or just let Thérèse herself read their hearts and bless them by her presence. The prayerful and constant line of pilgrims – young and old, the sick and people in wheelchairs – were often visibly moved as they stood in silence to touch, and be touched by, the grace of that very special moment.

St Thérèse referred to herself as a 'little flower', and the flower most associated with her is, of course, the rose. Roses were in abundance everywhere; people brought them to be blessed, placed them against the casket or carried them as an expression of their devotion and love for the saint.

The Reliquary

Perhaps the question most often asked during the pilgrimage was: 'What is in the casket?' The answer is very simple: some of the bones of St Thérèse of Lisieux. St Thérèse's body was not incorrupt, though her Carmelite habit and a palm branch placed in her hands were perfectly preserved. The bones or relics of the saint are enclosed in a Reliquary, 400 lb in weight, 5 ft long and 3 ft wide. It is a beautiful composition of polished jacaranda wood, decorated with exquisite gold and silver filigree and permanently mounted on a wooden tray. For security, the whole Reliquary is covered with a clear plexiglas cover. At every location, the Reliquary was placed in a prominent position, so that it was easily seen and readily accessible to all.

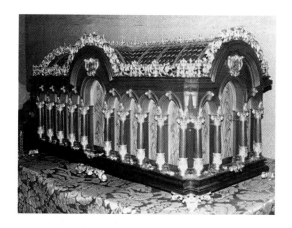

The Reliquary travelled around Ireland in what was affectionately known as the 'Thérèsemobile', a specially converted Mercedes Sprinter. This was beautifully designed and decorated as a portable shrine, with the simple words, 'The Sacred Relics of St Thérèse of Lisieux', inscribed on it.

Why Relics?

The use of relics goes back to the time of the apostles. 'So remarkable were the miracles worked by God at Paul's hands, that handkerchiefs or aprons which had touched him were taken to the sick and they were cured of their illnesses' (Acts 19:11-12). During a visit to Rome, St Thérèse herself wrote: 'all the pilgrims wanted to touch the tombs of the saints with their rosaries'.

It is only natural that people should treasure what is associated with the dead. The correct veneration of relics looks beyond what is material to the life of the saint. Veneration is not paid to relics as such, but to the saint they represent. Through them we feel physically and spiritually present to that person. Their lives point our hearts and our minds beyond themselves to God, the source of every grace and blessing.

The Beginning

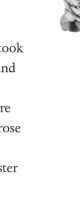

It was a simple start to an epic journey. At 4pm on Spy Wednesday, 11 April, Pat Sweeney drove the converted silver Mercedes Sprinter onto the *MV Normandy* at Rosslare Harbour. Also on board was a small party of 'pilgrims', led by Fr Linus Ryan, O Carm, National Coordinator of the Organising Committee, who were on their way to Lisieux to collect the Relics of St Thérèse of Lisieux, 'the greatest saint of modern times'. They were the guests of Irish Ferries and were welcomed on board by Captain Thomas Sarsfield.

The group arrived in Lisieux on Thursday morning, and later that day the Relics were formally handed over to Fr Ryan by Père Raymond Zambelli, Rector of the Lisieux Shrine, and Most Rev Guy Gaucher, Carmelite Bishop of Lisieux, with a simple exchange of greeting and a short service of prayer. It was fitting that RTÉ's Joe Duffy was there to relay the historic event to his listeners in Ireland, as it was the *Liveline* programme, more than anything else, that caused such a nationwide explosion of interest in the coming of the Relics.

On Saturday morning, the Thérèsemobile made its way to Cherbourg, escorted by *Gendarme* Jean-Michel Jeslin. Crew-members carried the Reliquary to a beautifully prepared room. Veneration of the Relics took place by the crew and by seven hundred and thirty-six passengers and lasted till 11pm, when the Relics were placed under the care of the ship's Master of Arms. As the sun rose on that historic Easter Sunday, the ship's auditorium was packed for the special Easter Mass, celebrated by Fr Ryan. As the *Normandy* neared the coast, the Rosslare lifeboat arrived to escort it into port. Already the crowd had gathered on the shore and all along the hills of Wexford. History was unfolding before their eyes. St Thérèse of Lisieux was coming and Ireland was ready. The long wait was over.

Céad Míle Fáilte

The 'Rose Revolution' is how Bishop Brendan Comiskey of Ferns described the long-awaited moment when the Relics of St Thérèse of Lisieux finally arrived in Ireland on Easter Sunday, 15 April 2001. This extraordinary event was witnessed by over fifteen thousand people from all over the country: enclosed Carmelite nuns – St Thérèse's own sisters – Carmelite friars, and friends and devotees of St Thérèse from every part of Ireland, amazed at the incredible event taking place in the usually quiet seaside town of Rosslare.

The arrival of St Thérèse, as the most important passenger on the ferry that morning, was the focus of an extraordinary sense of anticipation and celebration. The Reliquary was carried from the ferry by the Irish Army Ceremonial Unit from the Curragh, and transferred to the specially designed vehicle, popularly known as the 'Thérèsemobile'.

In welcoming St Thérèse to Wexford and to Ireland, Bishop Brendan outlined the principal purpose of this 'Pilgrimage of Grace', this 'once-in-a-lifetime visit': 'To remind us of the Easter message and to recall the gospel truth of God's unconditional love for his people. We are in the presence of sheer goodness and love and Thérèse's journey around Ireland will be a time of great joy, celebration and renewal.'

We bless you, Lord, for revealing the mystery of your kingdom to mere children. As we welcome the Relics of little Thérèse to our church, we give thanks to God who gives us such witnesses to guide us along our pilgrim way. (Prayer of Welcome)

Along the Way

Out of the Mouths of Babes

Catherine, a single parent, was explaining to her twelve-year-old son, David, that the casket was like a coffin and the whole ceremony in some way resembled a funeral. 'If that's so,' David replied, 'it's the happiest funeral I ever saw!'

Jimmy, who admitted he came only out of curiosity, was startled by the number of people he saw everywhere: 'I couldn't believe I was in a Catholic church,' he said, 'there were so many people and they all looked so happy!'

One Carmelite, travelling with the Reliquary, was a little taken aback when a young girl innocently asked him: 'Are you the relic?'

A father was telling his eight-year-old daughter that St Thérèse had come down from heaven to do good on earth. 'And when it's all over,' the young girl asked, 'how will she get back in again?'

Mobile Bookshop

A familiar sight at each venue was the white Mobile Bookshop, set up by the Organising Committee, to make available good background literature on St Thérèse. Ray Snowdon, from Kildare, expertly negotiated the 34 ft bus through narrow church gates, tight car parks and winding country roads. The Bookshop itself was managed by Una Barrett from Dublin, and the souvenir department by Philomena Queally from Dungarvan. To the great joy of all involved, the best-selling item was St Thérèse's own autobiography, *Story of a Soul*.

It would be impossible to over-emphasise the part played by the Gardaí during the nation-wide tour of the Relics. Everywhere they were courteous, efficient and professional. They were supportive of local committees preparing for the visit and, at every location, took control of the traffic and facilitated the vast crowds of people that came along. They also escorted the Thérèsemobile from one venue to another.

Garda Declan Egan and Garda Mick Walsh were on duty for the visit to Merrion. 'We all looked on it as a privilege and an honour to escort the Thérèsemobile,' Garda Declan Egan said, speaking for so many of his colleagues. 'It was great to be involved in such a historic event. There was such a feel-good factor and such positive vibes everywhere, it was great to be part of it.'

Fr John Keating, O Carm prepared the liturgical booklet used at all venues during the visit of St Thérèse. It contained a Service of Welcome and one of Farewell, with readings, prayers of intercession and a list of suitable hymns. The booklet also included Morning and Evening Prayer of the Church, various Masses for St Thérèse and special Liturgies for Children. It was an invaluable resource book for all host organisers and added to the spirit of reverence and prayerfulness that characterised the ceremonies at each location.

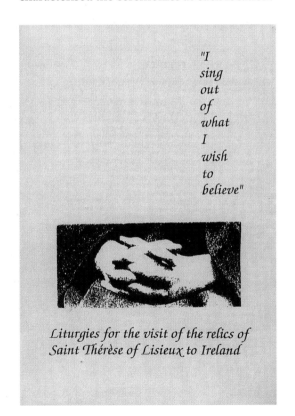

"I sing out of what I wish to believe"

Liturgies for the visit of the relics of Saint Thérèse of Lisieux to Ireland

A Young Saint

Many people were surprised by the extraordinary numbers of young people, all over Ireland, who came to visit the Relics of St Thérèse. Yet Thérèse herself is a young saint and speaks to young people in a way few adults can. They obviously felt they could relate to her: she was one of them and could understand their struggles and questioning. 'Her visit has done more for me in one day than all the talk and teaching about religion I heard at school,' said eighteen-year-old Tania from Wexford. Young people seemed especially attracted to the Night Vigil and it became a familiar sight to see them sitting cross-legged on the floor, their eyes closed, surrounded by the gentle glow of candles and listening to the soft music of the guitars. They were 'at home' with Thérèse and, there is no doubt, her presence was near and very real for them.

One of the Family

As St Thérèse's visit progressed throughout the land, it was extraordinary how much she became part of people's lives and was spoken of in such a natural and familiar way. 'Is that her wee house?' an old lady in Belfast wanted to know. 'She's one of us and she's welcome here any day,' a resident in St Theresa Gardens announced. 'After all, aren't we called after her?' But perhaps the tears in the eyes of the gardener in one of the convents expressed it best of all: 'When I lifted her into the silver van and saw her going off down the avenue, it was like saying goodbye to one of the family.'

The Night Watch

One of the most successful aspects of the 'Pilgrimage of Grace' was the enormous response to the Night Vigils. All over the country, churches remained open as veneration continued throughout the night. Many people preferred the small hours of the morning, savouring the silence and the quiet time of personal prayer with Thérèse. Often the Night Vigil was preceded by a midnight Mass and ended with a dawn Mass. 'This was the most precious period of the visit for me,' one lady said, 'I came on several nights to different churches. It was the silence and stillness that spoke to me most.' 'Who would think that a nun from Lisieux who died over a hundred years ago would keep so many people out of bed into the small hours of the morning,' Fr Paddy McClafferty from Belfast mused, 'and for the best of reasons!'

The Diary

April 15 Children only!

Over four thousand people gathered in St Aidan's Cathedral, Enniscorthy, to celebrate the arrival of St Thérèse. The cathedral itself was beautifully adorned with floral bouquets, banners, flags and bunting, as parishioners of all ages – young and old, toddlers, teenagers, the sick and the infirm – came to venerate St Thérèse. They stood reverently, queueing patiently to place their hands upon the ornate wooden casket, to pause for prayer and press a flower against the Reliquary.

There was a wonderful sense of familiarity and community in St Aidan's, as delighted and curious children gathered around Bishop Brendan, who humorously told the congregation: 'Only children are allowed to touch the Relics – but children of all ages!' He added, 'There are no expectations of this visit. What we need most of all is to trigger the imagination of people and to stay in touch with God, whether in church or in our homes, when we kneel down in the morning or at night. Thérèse will point the way. If God is working in our hearts, he will transform us.'

Breda Murphy and Ann Summers from Enniscorthy, who visited the Relics, were in no way surprised at the extraordinary response. 'People are speaking with their feet,' they said, 'and it is lovely to see the bishop, priests and people all mixing together. There is a deep search for leadership, at every level. Thérèse is a good model, especially for the young, struggling with their own beliefs. She was so young herself and her life was so simple.'

The Wonder of Wexford

In scenes never witnessed before in the county, huge crowds of people gathered to be part of something very special, the visit of St Thérèse of Lisieux to Wexford. The wonder in children's eyes, the watchful gaze of old ladies, and a general air of excitement showed that something truly extraordinary was unfolding in the historic town.

As the Thérèsemobile reached the top of Hill Street and turned into John Street, the crowds began to converge in ever-increasing numbers. Over five thousand people joined the procession to Bride Street Church, led by the local band, members of Wexford Corporation, a guard of honour formed by the local Pike Men, together with the Sisters of Perpetual Adoration who made a rare public appearance to welcome the Relics. A trumpet fanfare greeted the Reliquary as it entered the sanctuary, and the church bells rang out around the town.

As dawn broke, the Army carried the Reliquary by torchlight procession to the convent of the Adoration Sisters where the community had the privilege of a short period of veneration. The final stop took place in Rowe Street Church, where Bishop Comiskey celebrated Mass.

Local curate, Fr Jim Fegan, was deeply moved. 'In all my years in Wexford I have

April 16 & 17

never seen such a positive response. There is much talk about the decline in faith in Ireland today but it certainly wasn't evident here in Wexford. It was wonderful to see people expressing their faith in such a spontaneous way. We wanted everyone to enjoy the visit of St Thérèse and they certainly seem to have done so.'

Rose O'Neill was one of those waiting patiently to visit the Relics. 'Thérèse was part of our family;

her picture was always hanging in the same spot. When I was expecting, my husband said, "If it's a girl we'll call her Thérèse." And we did.'

On the way to New Ross, the Thérèsemobile made a brief stop at St Mary's Church, Cushinstown, where over a thousand people had gathered to venerate the Relics and witness the special blessing by Bishop Brendan Comiskey of a new statue of St Thérèse, to be erected in the church grounds in memory of this special day.

Candles Glowing in the Night

The Three Bullet Pike Group formed a colourful guard of honour around the Thérèsemobile as it approached New Ross. Outside the church, crowds had already gathered to witness the solemn moment as the casket was carried shoulder-high into the sanctuary. So began a day which 'I personally will never forget,' said Bishop Brendan Comiskey, describing the event as he spoke to the massive congregation gathered for the occasion. It was the largest public expression of faith ever witnessed in the town.

The highlight of the visit to New Ross was undoubtedly the transfer of the Reliquary by candlelight procession from the parish church to the Carmelite convent overlooking the historic town. The New Ross and District Pipe Band led the procession, followed by the Urban District Council and Civil Defence. All along the street, candles burned brightly as thousands followed the Thérèsemobile in the fading evening light. There followed a night of treasured memories for all who came to venerate. The chapel had never seen such a flow of pilgrims. The Carmelite sisters themselves were amazed that 'one of their own' could attract such an outpouring of devotion, reverence and joy.

April 18

Once in a Lifetime

The banner, 'Gorey Welcomes St Thérèse', was raised high above the crowd as the Thérèsemobile arrived into the town. Men and women, young and old, huddled in groups around the 1798 monument. Candle-bearers, rows of school children and various groups joined with local people who watched in amazement as the silver van, led by a lone piper, made the slow journey to the parish church. Fr John O'Reilly said he was delighted with the response. Reflecting something that was already becoming a notable feature of the visit, he commented on the 'amazing age profile'. 'Given the average age at most Sunday Masses now, I expected the same to be true here, but nothing could be further from the truth. It is amazing to see so many young people visiting the Relics.'

'It's great for Gorey,' said Peg Sheridan, one of the many flower-holders. 'I wouldn't have missed this for the whole world.' Nellie Breen was also there, holding two red roses, one for herself and *one for her sister in Manchester. 'I have always had a wonderful devotion to the Little Flower. We would never get a chance like this again.'*

When the Thérèsemobile pulled up, Margaret and her daughter Noeleen, a child with Down's Syndrome, knelt in silent prayer. Then they stood, clutching hands, as the procession moved down the main street.

After the reception of the Relics by Bishop Brendan Comiskey, up to fifteen thousand people from north Wexford and south Wicklow venerated the Relics throughout the night and the next morning.

As the Reliquary left Gorey, people followed it to the very end of the town, reluctant to see her go.

En route to Knocktopher, the Reliquary made a brief stop at the historic church of St Aidan's, Ferns, for a short Service of Prayer and veneration.

St Thérèse Superstar!

'Thérèse Superstar' was how the *Irish Farmers Journal* captured the visit of St Thérèse of Lisieux to the Carmelite priory at Knocktopher, Co Kilkenny. Scenes never witnessed before unfolded dramatically as the Little Flower was welcomed by Fr Peter Kehoe, O Carm, her Carmelite brothers and the people of the parish. Pictures of the young saint adorned the church, candles glowed in her honour and there were hundreds of roses and floral arrangements everywhere. Every available seat and standing-space was occupied, as people eagerly gathered for this momentous occasion – a day that will never be forgotten in the history of the parish and in the Carmelite annals of Knocktopher. The church was filled to over-flowing for the evening Mass, the special midnight Mass and the early-morning 'workers' Mass'. There was also a Service of Healing, and the night veneration was interspersed with prayers, music and readings from St Thérèse.

As one parishioner described it, 'It is something we never thought would happen and I'm sure we will never see again.'

On Wednesday, 18 April the children of Ballyhale National School and Knocktopher Vocational School came together in the friary church to perform a delightful musical presentation of the life and message of St Thérèse. The children were very much at home in expressing the joy and youthfulness of Thérèse through song and music, and the readings from Story of a Soul *were accompanied by the choirs from Our Lady of Mount Carmel Church and the parish of Mullinavat. The entire production was written and directed by Vivian Teigh.*

April 20 A Saint for All Ages

Even though it became commonplace later on, Kilkenny was the first place to see long queues of people lining the streets into the early hours of the morning. It was also the first time it became clear just how wide and varied the age groups were going to be: people from nine to ninety were already in evidence around St Mary's Cathedral.

'The visit went beyond all our expectations,' said Fr Oliver Maher, who described the experience as essentially one of prayerful devotion. 'So many people,' he added, 'so attentive, quiet and reverential.'

Kilkenny was the first venue to host the liturgical pageant, Shower of Roses, *an original interpretation of the life of St Thérèse, written and directed by Martina Lehane. The production – a visually exciting interplay of song, drama, music and dance – was musically directed by Tina Hurley. Thérèse's life is beautifully linked with the gospel story of Jesus' own life, giving the music a contemporary ring and challenge, especially for young people in search of their own identity. The whole performance was a wonderful expression of youthful energy, haunting melodies and lively, happy voices. 'Thérèse's unique strength of character and resilience are her most impressive attributes,' said Martina, 'and are at the very core of the production. Thérèse has a ring of truth about her; hers is not an unattainable holiness. There is something real, ordinary, and very human about her.'* Shower of Roses *was performed to packed audiences in several venues throughout the country, on every occasion to a standing ovation.*

A **Shower of Roses**

A touring production based on the life and interpreted message of St. Thérèse of Liseux. Visually exciting, it interweaves music, mime and dance.

… is an original interpretation directed by Martina Lehane.
Musically directed by Tina Hurley

April 21   Merciful Love

The eve of Low Sunday, feast of Divine Mercy, was an appropriate day for St Thérèse, the apostle of Merciful Love, to make her first visit to a Dublin Carmel. For Sr Noeleen, one of the Kilmacud community, it was a double joy, as she was celebrating her Silver Jubilee of Profession that same day. The front door was too narrow for the casket, and even the back doors had to be specially widened for the visit. But it was a picturesque sight to see the lines of Cubs and Beavers forming a guard of honour as the Reliquary was carried aloft by the young Venture Scouts through the convent garden, into the nuns' choir. But not only were doors widened, hearts also were thrown open as the sisters and people joined together in venerating the Relics and in the celebration of Evening and Morning Prayer and each of the special Masses.

The gospels came alive as so many sick and infirm people were tenderly carried and wheeled towards the Reliquary with expectant faith. It was also lovely to see the First Communion children in white form a guard of honour around the casket in the afternoon. The Night Vigil was marked by the large number of young people – Friends of Calcutta, Youth 2000, university students – who performed a graceful 'Liturgy of Love' around the Reliquary, and sang and prayed with such heartfelt reverence throughout the night, climaxing in a beautiful dawn Mass.

Siobhan Greally had travelled from Rathmines to visit St Thérèse. She had a very special reason for doing so. 'I had breast cancer six years ago and was so depressed and frightened that I hardly believed in anything. While I was in hospital an elderly nun came to visit me. She told me the story of St Thérèse and gave me her prayer-card. She also said she would do a novena for me. My heart wasn't in it but I prayed to her each night anyway and somehow I got through the experience and have been cancer-free for three years now. I don't think you can doubt the power of St Thérèse or of God himself when you come through an experience like that.'

Roses for Thérèse

April 22

The Carmelite church in Beaumont was the first parish in Dublin to receive the Relics of St Thérèse. Much planning and not a little worry had gone into the preparation for the visit. It was, after all, the first, so it was difficult to know for certain what to expect. In the end, everything went off perfectly. Over forty thousand people, of all ages, came to venerate this 'greatest saint of modern times'. It was edifying to see the patience with which the people waited, sometimes in the rain, for their turn to venerate the Relics. Many people were visibly moved as they placed a rose on the Reliquary, which would become a treasured possession for a long time to come. 'It was a humbling experience,' said Fred Haslem, Chairman of Beaumont Parish Council, 'to see so many young people, many with babies in their arms, coming to the casket with such obvious devotion.' On Monday morning, the school children returned from their Easter holidays, and came in force to visit this little saint who has such an appeal for young people.

'It can hardly be put into words,' said Fr Patrick Staunton, O Carm, Parish Priest of Beaumont: 'The visit of St Thérèse to our parish has been a truly unforgettable and uplifting experience. We are all especially delighted with the high numbers of young people who have turned up. Thérèse has an obvious attraction for them – after all, she was young herself and never lost her own youthful spirit.'

Ten-year-old Declan Casey came with his mother, Eileen, and younger brother, David. 'Our teachers told us about the visit of St Thérèse and we brought her roses and pictures that we made in school.' His mother added, 'Both my parents always had a great devotion to St Thérèse, and the picture in our house is the one my mother had for many years. It's very precious to our family and I brought it here today to touch the Relics.'

It was obvious that Beaumont was the start of something big.

April 23   Fáilte to St Thérèse

Sunshine and a large crowd greeted the arrival of the Relics of St Thérèse at the Carmelite convent, Roebuck. The Thérèsemobile halted between the ranks of soldiers who formed a guard of honour and carried the Reliquary into the convent. Pupils from the nearby Our Lady's Grove School, holding roses and a large banner, 'Fáilte to St Thérèse', sang a specially-composed hymn, *Mission of Love*, during the reception. In the evening, Bishop Martin Drennan gave a talk on St Thérèse, which was followed by Night Prayer. The chapel was never empty during the all-night Vigil and, for Morning Prayer and Mass which followed, the congregation filled the nuns' choir and overflowed into the convent grounds. More school children arrived with their teachers during the morning to sing hymns and venerate the Relics. Some patients from the Central Mental Hospital, Dundrum, also came for a brief Prayer Service with their chaplain.

Before the soldiers carried the Reliquary to the waiting Thérèsemobile, they asked for a brief moment to themselves, to stand in quiet reverence around the casket. Never was silence more eloquent, as their simple gesture expressed the gratitude and respect of soldiers, at home and abroad, to the 'little saint' who had befriended so many of their companions in the trenches.

Sandra Casey and her husband, Barry, had a special reason for coming to visit the Relics. Their five-year-old granddaughter, Louise, was knocked down by a car a year ago and had severe head injuries. She was in intensive care for two months. 'We thought we were going to lose her; we stayed by her bedside day and night, praying very hard. My mother always had great devotion to the Little Flower, so the whole family did a novena to her. Louise recovered fully without any sign of brain damage. Thank God, she is now healthy and happy. We brought her here today to say thanks and we hope Louise herself will grow to love Thérèse as much as we do.'

Up with the Dawn!

One of the highest single figures of the tour to date was recorded during the visit of the Relics to Carlow. Even some of the shops closed for the arrival. The Thérèsemobile arrived at Shamrock Square from where it was escorted by a guard of honour along Tullow Street and College Street to the Cathedral of the Assumption. Here it was welcomed by Bishop Laurence Ryan and by a sea of delighted faces. The cathedral was filled to overflowing for the evening Mass, and a continuous wave of people made their way to the cathedral for veneration, well into the early hours of the morning. A unique feature of the visit was the presence of spiritual counsellors who were available throughout the day.

Fr Gerard Ahern was absolutely delighted with the marvellous level of interest. 'People had their alarm clocks set for three o'clock in the morning,' he said, 'to make sure they did not miss the visit of Thérèse!'

Marian and her friend, Anne, came to Carlow for the day. Their joy was evident as they left the church clutching a beautiful bouquet of yellow roses which had just touched the Reliquary. Both women have a life-long devotion to Thérèse and were thrilled at the events unfolding before their eyes. 'As a young girl I always kept St Thérèse's prayer-card and prayed to her every day,' Marian said. 'So many people have left the church for whatever reason; Thérèse will help restore their faith and remind them once again of God's love and mercy.'

A Healing Touch

The visit to St James' Hospital – one of the largest in Dublin, with a thousand beds and three thousand staff – proved to be a particularly moving experience. The four Carmelite chaplains received the Relics, while nurses and staff formed a guard of honour. A vast array of visitors came to venerate the Relics in the beautifully decorated hospital chapel. Many of the visitors were anxious relatives praying for their loved ones who lay in nearby hospital beds, others were patients themselves seeking the intercession of St Thérèse for strength and healing.

During the visit of the Relics, all the patients in the hospital were blessed. Hospital staff venerated the Relics throughout the night. Before departure, the Relics were brought to Hospital Ward 4, a large geriatric unit, where the patients are largely immobile, and they were thrilled with the opportunity to venerate the Relics for one hour. Fr Bernard Murphy, O Carm, Head Chaplain, was extremely pleased with the response and with the marvellous support and help given by the hospital authorities, who spared no effort to make the visit so successful. Nevertheless, he could not deny that the visit was also a poignant one for himself and his colleagues, as the Carmelites are about to leave St James' Hospital after one hundred and forty years of service as chaplains.

Timothy Murphy was visiting his mother, Bridie, a patient in St James' for the past week, and was waiting his turn to venerate the Relics and to have a special rose blessed for his mother. 'Before this happened,' he said, 'she had been planning to visit the Relics with my sister but got sick suddenly. She has a strong devotion to the Little Flower and now feels Thérèse has come here today to see her and help her get well.'

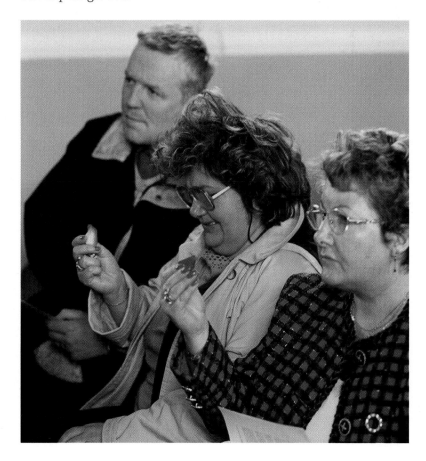

April 26 & 27

Grace-Filled Days

'Grace-filled days in Gracepark Road' was how one lady neatly summed up the two-day visit of St Thérèse to Hampton. The visit had a double focus, as Hampton is home not only to the Carmelite community, but also to the Theresian Trust, founded in 1984 by Maurice and Christine Frost, to promote the message and teaching of St Thérèse. Gracepark Road itself was festively adorned with bunting and banners, and the grounds looked splendid as flags and decorations fluttered in the afternoon breeze. Girls from the local school stood in line as the Reliquary arrived and was carried to the chapel door by students from All Hallows College. Mother Prioress and the community were there to welcome their sister, St Thérèse, together with members of the 'Friends of Hampton' and representatives of the Theresian Trust. Many were visibly moved as the nuns themselves wheeled the Reliquary into the sanctuary and led the congregation in the readings and prayers of the Opening Ceremony.

During the two-day visit, local groups took turns in leading prayers and providing music for the veneration, and many were delighted to join the community for the recitation of the Prayer of the Church. There was a special welcome for the large group from Blanchardstown parish, as the nuns had spent thirty years there before moving to Hampton. For many, the highlight of the visit was the Vigil and midnight Mass organised by the Young Adults' Taizé Group from the Pro-Cathedral. A deeply prayerful atmosphere prevailed; the chapel and choir were aglow with candles as the Vigil was interspersed with readings from St Thérèse, meditations, chants and periods of quiet prayer.

'Someone everyone can relate to' was how sixteen-year-old Claire Sweeney described St Thérèse of Lisieux. 'I don't know very much about saints but she is one I'm interested in. She was very young and went through the same things as young people of my age. I know she lived in another time, but in many ways she is very much like young people today and I find that amazing. To see the crowds today is incredible. You'd wonder what they are all searching for.'

April 28

tremendous atmosphere of joy and celebration throughout the visit, helped by the prayerful music and singing of the Order's own Columban Choir.

A Village Celebrates

Everyone wanted to be involved, people working together with good humour and great energy. There was a sense that Thérèse's own spirit was hovering over the beautiful village of Delgany – the only place in the 'Garden County' to have the privilege of hosting the Relics. By the time the Thérèsemobile arrived at the Carmelite convent, everything was in place: the church grounds were floodlit, tents and banners erected, and the place buzzing with excitement. The bells of both the Church of

Although the visit of the Reliquary to the oratory of the Knights of St Columbanus in Ely Place was only three hours long, the crowds which came exceeded all expectations. According to Supreme Knight, Niall Kennedy, the experience was 'one of the most moving of my life'. There was a

Ireland and the convent rang out in unison a message of welcome.

The Reception was simple and dignified, with the help of a lone piper, the FCA, the local camogie team, flower-girls, and musicians from Mater Dei Institute. The Reliquary was placed in the small, beautifully decorated convent chapel. People came from all over the county, and veneration continued all during the twenty-two hours' visit. Over a hundred people walked in pilgrimage from the parish of Kilcoole and prayed in deep silence around the Reliquary. Some felt it was a 'little miracle' that the original supply of roses, reserved for the sick, never ran out. As these were distributed, others replaced them. The morning Eucharist was a most joyous celebration, with so many people present.

As the Thérèsemobile left the convent, the local GAA formed a guard of honour and people lined the streets. The Church of Ireland service finished in time to allow the congregation to join their Catholic neighbours on the streets of Delgany.

On reflection, one sister summed up in verse the experience of so many:

> Thérèse,
> Your spirit hovered over each heart
> And sparked into flame something
>   unexplainable
> Or was it simply Love?
> Oh! not any love if love can be reduced
> But a spark of God's Maternal Love
> And we caught Fire.

April 29

A Foretaste of Heaven

Gort Muire, by reason of its location, is somewhat removed from the main thoroughfare, but people found their way from the surrounding parishes and beyond. The crowds continued to pour in during the afternoon and night hours. There was an extraordinary atmosphere of peace and contemplation in the chapel, which enticed many people to linger on and pray. Roses specially flown in from Holland were very much in demand, as was anything to do with the saint: prayer-cards, publications and images. Students from St Tiernan's College helped with the stewarding and kept the traffic on the move. The

Carmelite community had assembled at the entrance gate, escorting the Thérèsemobile up the avenue. Already there was a large queue of people stretching from the chapel to the end of the front building. A group from Terenure College Senior Rugby Team, current holders of the Leinster Cup, carried the Relics into the chapel where they were received by Fr Billy Langan, O Carm and the welcoming songs of the community. Special provision was made for the disabled and people in wheelchairs. The Knights of Malta gladly gave of their time and expertise.

Nothing interfered with the tranquil flow of people venerating the Relics. It was as if they were meeting an old friend as they touched the Reliquary with bare hands, pressed a rose against the glass or raised up a baby. There were lots of babies in arms. At 11 o'clock that night, the Office of Compline was celebrated with a church full of people. That was a climactic moment, a foretaste of heaven.

Next morning, people began to pour in again until the 11 o'clock Mass which was packed, many people having to stand in the corridors. In his homily, Fr Brian McKay, O Carm highlighted Thérèse's relevance for so many of life's situations today. A guard of honour from St Tiernan's lined the avenue for the departure. Thérèse still had many miles to travel but there was a palpable air of sadness as she left.

'Roses for Blessing!'

The Pro-Cathedral, just off Dublin's main thoroughfare, was a hive of activity, with crowds gathering from early morning to catch a glimpse of the Reliquary as it arrived. The adjoining streets were blocked by the throngs of people, but no one seemed to mind on such a joyous occasion. Many carried prayer-cards, roses and medals to place against the casket while the famous Dublin street-sellers wheeled their prams up and down, selling 'Roses for Blessing'. Special Prayer Services took place in the evening, while various groups from surrounding parishes kept vigil throughout the night.

At the farewell Mass on Tuesday morning, Cardinal Desmond Connell spoke of St Thérèse's love for, and identification with, Christ as expressed in her devotion to the Holy Face. He also mentioned the joy that the visit of St Thérèse had brought to the archdiocese. 'She has obviously struck a special chord in the hearts of the Dublin people,' he said.

Rosaleen Delaney was first in the queue. 'I've been living in Dublin for forty years and always pray to St Thérèse. I have never seen such crowds here or felt so peaceful. It was lovely to see so many good people praying together. Dublin should be proud of St Thérèse and grateful for what she's doing for the country.'

May 1

Visit of a Lifetime

'The visit of a lifetime' was how the Carmelite nuns themselves described the 'never-to-be-forgotten day' when their sister, Thérèse of Lisieux, came to visit the beautiful Convent of St Joseph's in the seaside village of Malahide. The parishes of the Fingal deanery, together with a vast team of helpers and volunteers, were involved in the weeks of preparation and organisation. The pretty village looked its best, gaily decked for the day; a specially designed floral Cross in the centre of Malahide added to the sense of occasion. Shops closed for the first two hours of the visit. Pupils from the local primary and secondary schools lined the route as the Thérèsemobile arrived. On a bright May afternoon, the beauty of the convent was enhanced by the magnificent flowers, which were in abundance everywhere. One of the thoughtful touches of the visit was the use of buggies, supplied by Malahide's golf club, to bring the older people up the steep hill. The large number visiting the Relics surpassed all expectations and added to the sense of joy and celebration that prevailed.

Anne Tower was in Malahide. 'Thérèse has a great way of communicating with people of all ages,' she said. 'I've asked for her help down through the years for my family and my children and I've really been blessed. She is the greatest flower of them all.'

May 2

Shake Hands with Thérèse!

The Legion of Mary was founded by Frank Duff in Dublin in 1921, just four years before St Thérèse was canonised. She is one of the most popular saints in the spirituality of the Legion of Mary, and indeed her own missionary zeal is reflected in the great apostolic tradition of the Legion. It was, then, an occasion of special joy when the Relics of St Thérèse visited the Headquarters of the Legion of Mary in Brunswick Street near the Dublin Liberties.

The complex includes the Central Office of the Legion, the Morning Star Hostel for men and the Regina Coeli Hostel for women. The whole street was colourfully decked with bunting and banners, while the Papal and French flags fluttered gently in the wind. The large crowd was cheerful and enthusiastic. Little wonder that, in such a relaxed and friendly atmosphere, one little lad wanted to know if he could shake hands with St Thérèse!

May 2

The Reliquary was carried up the hill by a guard of honour formed by members of the Legion, where the Papal Nuncio, Most Rev Giuseppe Lazzarotto, received it. Boys from Brunswick Street School sang a 'Céad Míle Fáilte' and the CIE choir led the whole congregation in a chorus of hymns. The first part of the veneration took place in the open air before starting its joyful procession to the little oratory, where the residents of both Hostels led the readings and prayers. The Papal Nuncio spoke of the importance of the message of St Thérèse for the world today: a message of great simplicity and one of trust and confidence in a God who is our loving Father.

Fr Joseph Moran, OP, National Director of the Legion of Mary, celebrated Mass in the evening for the residents and staff of the Legion, as well as for members of the general public. President Mary McAleese and her family were also present at the Mass.

Sharon from Monkstown had been looking forward to this day for some time. 'I stayed here a few years ago with my two-year-old boy and things were bad then. I'm back on my feet now and wanted to thank Thérèse – she suffered like all of us and shows how we can overcome it.'

The Happiest Day of All

St Thérèse made no secret of the fact that her school-days were 'the saddest years' of her life and that her memories of boarding school were indeed 'very painful'. What a delight it must have been for her, then, to see the smiling faces of a thousand boys in the Carmelite College, Terenure, who formed an impressive guard of honour along the avenue as the Thérèsemobile arrived. The boys were also very much involved in the Welcoming Ceremony, taking part in the readings and prayers of intercession, while the voices of the combined senior and junior choirs joyfully rang out in the beautifully decorated chapel. The college grounds looked splendid in the afternoon sunshine and provided ample park-ing-space for the thousands of visitors who came along, supervised and coordinated by pupils from the senior school. The spacious college chapel facilitated the continuous stream of people who came, day and night, throughout the visit. Overall, it was a marvellous historic occasion, not just for the Carmelite community and the pupils, but surely a happy school-experience for St Thérèse herself!

Twenty-four-year-old Sarah Harrison came to visit and described her experience as 'peaceful and calming'. 'I'd never really heard of St Thérèse before but I just couldn't believe the crowds and wanted to see what it was all about. She was only my age when she died and I'd like to learn more about her. I'm glad I came – everyone seems so happy and there's a great atmosphere.'

May 4

St Thérèse behind bars

It was possibly the most moving stop of the nationwide journey to date. St Thérèse's visit to Mountjoy Prison offered an emotional and enlightening insight into a world behind bars. The twenty-two-hour visit was an incredible experience and a proud and momentous day for the one-hundred-and-fifty-year-old prison, the staff and seven hundred prisoners. The visit was prepared for with meticulous planning and a notable air of reverence and dignity. On this special occasion, all were equal and all were welcome. A team of prison officers placed the 400 lb casket on a specially designed machine, slowly raising it to the upper level, where it could be adequately accommodated in the beautifully prepared church, adorned with flowers and candle-holders made that very week by the prisoners.

A steady stream of both staff and prisoners visited the church throughout the course of

the day to venerate the Relics. During the afternoon, a number of the Carmelite priests spoke to the prisoners about St Thérèse and prayed with them. In the evening, a special Mass was held for the staff of Mountjoy and their families, celebrated by Mountjoy Prison chaplain, Fr Declan Blake – a really joyous and uplifting occasion. 'When St Thérèse spoke of her life in the convent as "a happy imprisonment", she obviously was not referring to Mountjoy!', Fr Philip Brennan, O Carm said in his homily. 'But her words are a reminder to us today that we all live in some kind of prison and we need to unlock so much in our hearts that is unfree and hinders us from a greater love.'

Governor of the prison, John Lonergan, was delighted with the success of the event. 'Most of the prison population came and I believe that they found something special. Particularly in the context of a prison – I think it is most appropriate for someone like Thérèse to be here, who felt such compassion for the marginalised. She certainly brought peace here today and I hope it will have spin-off effects for a long time to come.'

A Visit of Hope

At 10 o'clock on Friday night, the Relics of St Thérèse were transferred to the Dóchas Centre, part of the Mountjoy building which houses seventy female prisoners. Assistant Governor, Catherine Comerford was there to

welcome the visitors and the women prisoners themselves who had worked hard to prepare for the event and to ensure everything went smoothly. Their personal involvement made the visit very meaningful. One of the women prisoners painted a beautiful picture of St Thérèse, against a background of a Cross and a rose; another designed a bright, welcoming banner, inscribed with the lines of their Vision Statement:

We are a community which embraces people's respect and dignity. We encourage personal growth and development in a caring and safe environment. We are committed to addressing the needs of each person in a healing and holistic way. We actively promote closer interaction with the wider community.

Most of the women attended an all-night Vigil, led by the Críost Linn Folk Group. The visit ended on Saturday morning with a Mass celebrated by the chaplain of the Dóchas Centre, Fr Eamonn Crosson. 'The word, "Dóchas" means "hope",' Fr Eamonn said, 'and a renewed sense of hope is precisely what many of the women here have found during this historic and very special visit.'

May 5

Broadcasting the Good News

The highlight of the visit of St Thérèse to St Colmcille's Carmelite church in Knocklyon was undoubtedly the televised Mass, which took place on Sunday, 6 May. This was a truly wonderful celebration, featuring, at the beginning, a historical presentation by Kairos Communications of the life and background of the saint. The whole celebration was enhanced by the glorious singing of the combined parish choirs, an inspiring homily by Fr

David Weakliam, O Carm, and a very moving post-Communion mime by the young people of the parish, to the music of the specially-composed song, *To Those who are Little*. Other services during the visit included a special Mass of Healing and Anointing of the Sick, and a midnight Mass which preceded the all-night Vigil. The RTÉ broadcast touched the lives of countless people, especially the sick and housebound who might not have had any other opportunity to experience the incredible impact of St Thérèse's visit to Ireland. Fr Anthony McDonald, O Carm was more than happy with the day. 'We had around four hundred volunteers giving their time and energy to make the visit such a success,' he said. 'It was wonderful to see so many people working together, making the event such a memorable one for our parish.'

Paddy and Carmel Neary will celebrate fifty years of wedded bliss on the feast-day of St Thérèse and for many of those years have been regular pilgrims to Lisieux. 'We started going there in the seventies and now our children and their families join us as well,' said Paddy. 'St Thérèse is someone you can talk to about anything; she is everyone's sister and everyone's friend and we feel she has helped us many times over the years.' Carmel agrees: 'To be here today is just incredible. We will probably go to some of the other venues as well and bring our grandchildren – they've heard us talking about her for long enough!'

Talking with Thérèse

It was a warm, sunny May Bank Holiday weekend as the Relics of St Thérèse arrived for a two-day visit to the Carmelite Retreat Centre in Donnybrook. The monastery grounds were tastefully decorated with flags and bunting, and a large crowd was waiting with the Carmelite community outside the church as the Thérèsemobile drew up. The Reliquary was received by the Prior, Fr Willie

Moran, OCD, and carried into the church by a guard of honour from Donnybrook Fire Station. There was a calm and prayerful atmosphere in the small church all during the visit, as people sat quietly close to the casket, relishing the quiet time talking with Thérèse.

In the afternoon, pupils from St Mary's School, Belmont, came for a special Prayer Service, which included readings from *Story of a Soul*. The Piccolo Lasso Choir also paid a beautiful musical tribute to Thérèse. The Carmelite Provincial, Fr Vincent O'Hara, was the principal celebrant at the evening Mass: 'Where Thérèse really scored was in her attitude,' he said, 'she expected great things from God and we now see that she was not mistaken. The only qualification she asks is a

May 6-8

heart open to love.' Chief celebrant at the Monday morning Mass was Bishop Martin Drennan, the ceremony enhanced by the music of well-known singer Carmel Boyle whose album, *White Wings and Roses*, is based on the poetry of St Thérèse. The parishioners of Donnybrook were special guests at a Mass later that evening, with Fr Pat Carroll, PP, the principal celebrant. The Avila Charismatic Prayer Group held an evening service that led into the midnight Mass and all-night Vigil.

The following morning, the Reliquary left Avila for a two-hour visit to the nearby Royal Hospital, where chaplain, Fr Enda Watters said Mass. This was a moving experience: a visit, however short, that brought immense joy and blessing to the patients and staff. 'A truly "royal" visit' was how one man expressed it.

One lady who came to visit St Thérèse in Avila was Anne Dempsey, who shared a great love for the Little Flower with her late husband, Robert, and together they visited Lisieux every year. 'I think the secret of Thérèse is her simplicity, that's really what her "Little Way" is all about.' Anne is convinced that Thérèse has had a big influence on the whole family. Her children also feel a certain bond with Thérèse: One day, a few years ago, her now grown-up daughter suddenly went very quiet and when she asked her if she was alright, she replied, 'Yes, Thérèse is talking to me.'

A Felt Presence

One of the most moving experiences of the Dublin itinerary was undoubtedly the short, unscheduled stopover at St Mary's Centre for the Visually Impaired on the Merrion Road. The Centre, run by the Irish Sisters of Charity, is home to some one hundred ladies who were overjoyed at the surprise visit of St Thérèse. It was a deeply moving experience to see the residents feeling their way around the casket, praying with their hands, reaching out in darkness to touch the Reliquary, their faces radiant with an inner light. 'I didn't know what to expect,' Nellie O'Mahony admitted, 'but when I placed my hand along the casket I felt a deep joy and peace, and I just whispered a prayer to the Little Flower and thanked her for coming to visit us.' Sr Gerard, who arranged the visit, was overjoyed: 'Sighted people can go out to one of the churches,' she said. 'It is not as easy for blind people to do so. There was a felt presence of God in the chapel during the veneration and tears of joy and happiness on so many faces.'

In the Heart of the City

St Teresa's Carmelite Church, Clarendon Street, is one of the best-known and most-frequented churches in Dublin. With the prime advantage of a city-centre location and a continual flow of visitors, it was no surprise that over forty thousand people came to Clarendon Street during the two-day visit of the saint. A large media contingent was present as the Thérèsemobile arrived, and the colourful rose-vendors added a touch of festivity to the occasion. An enthusiastic crowd had gathered by the time the Reliquary arrived, and it was received by the Prior, Fr Paul Dempsey, OCD and the Carmelite community. Throughout the day, people of all ages and backgrounds visited the church, many carrying roses and prayer-cards as they queued patiently for their opportunity to touch the Reliquary.

On the Thursday morning, Fr Paul celebrated a farewell Mass in the presence of a packed congregation with beautiful singing provided by the church choir. As the Relics left the church, the Tara Street Fire Brigade formed a guard of honour and proudly carried the Reliquary to the top end of Clarendon Street, to the rapturous applause and acclamation of the people – a fitting send-off for the great saint.

Seven-year-old Claire O'Connell was at St Teresa's with her mother and brought a beautiful bouquet of red roses and a picture of the saint she had made. 'We bought the flowers on the way for "the little saint",' she said. 'I'm making my First Holy Communion next week and I have a picture of St Thérèse at home when she was the same age as me. We learned all about her at school and drew pictures of her. She is very special because she talks to God for you, so you don't have to do it yourself.'

May 10

Thérèse Soldiers On!

Joan of Arc was one of Thérèse's favourite saints. She kept her picture in her prayer-book. She even wrote a play about her and, as if to make the relationship more real, acted the part herself, dressed in full military uniform. So, it was fitting that she should be guest of honour at the newly re-dedicated St Brigid's Garrison Church in the Curragh Camp, Kildare, where military ceremony is an everyday fact of life.

Sergeant-major Liam Cosgrave headed the official guard of honour consisting of the First Air Defence Regiment, joined by members of the Military Police and the Defence Forces Training Centre. Lone piper, Sgt David Usher's soulful playing of *The Curragh of Kildare* broke through the hush as the Reliquary was welcomed at the church door by the clergy and the military personnel, including Chief of Staff, Colm Mangan and GOC of the Defence Forces Training Centre,

Brigadier General Jim Saunderson. A fanfare *Ode to Joy*, from the DFTC Military Band, greeted the Reliquary as seven soldiers bore the Relics into the sanctuary.

Military chaplain, Fr P. J. McEvoy spoke of the significance of this day, given that Thérèse herself hailed from a military background. Both her maternal grandparents had had distinguished careers in the French army. 'The fact that such an ordinary and relatively unknown French girl has become one of the world's best-known and best-loved saints is an extraordinary phenomenon which cannot be explained in human terms, and stands as a powerful sign of God's presence in our world today. The significance of Thérèse's visit to this country cannot be overestimated. We need to touch and make contact with Thérèse, just as the woman in the gospel reached out and touched the cloak of Jesus. We are privileged and honoured and this is a grace-filled day for all of us,' he concluded.

A Sort of Homecoming

It was 'a sort of homecoming' for Kildare-born Fr Linus Ryan, O Carm, the Carmelite priest chiefly responsible for bringing the Reliquary to Ireland, when St Thérèse came to the White Abbey Carmelite church of Kildare. It was also a special day for three other local men: official driver of the Thérèsemobile, Pat Sweeney, his co-driver Jim Doyle and Ray Snowdon, driver of the Mobile Bookshop.

Kildare town itself was alive with excitement and anticipation. People crowded the church grounds to welcome the Thérèsemobile, while others took the wise step of securing a seat inside and were delighted to see Len Ryan, captain of the Kildare football team, and his sporting colleagues carry the casket to the steps of the church, accompanied by the music of the Newbridge Patrician School Band. A brief Prayer Service took place at the church door before the Relics were brought to the foot of the altar.

A constant stream of pilgrims came to venerate the Relics during the two-day visit, including busloads of disabled people, several in wheelchairs, who were always given immediate access to the Reliquary. A special feature, which caught the attention of many visitors, was the beautiful outdoor shrine to St Thérèse, ablaze with candles day and night. There was a marvellous spirit of hospitality evident throughout the visit, as the whole community came together to welcome and offer refreshments to all who came for the occasion.

On Friday morning, Fr Martin Ryan, O Carm was chief celebrant at a special concelebrated Mass for over seven hundred children from the local area. 'The message Thérèse most wanted to pass on,' Fr Ryan told the children, 'was the power of love, and this can be summed up effectively in just one phrase: "The love in your heart is not there to stay – love is not love till you give it away".'

Twenty-year-old Deirdre Austin travelled to Kildare town from Dublin especially to experience the atmosphere and spoke of her personal devotion to Thérèse, particularly since she was struck down by a debilitating illness some years ago. 'I was born on 1 October – her feast-day,' she smiled, 'and I was diagnosed with ME when I was thirteen. I had to give up school and I get very tired.'

Yet, despite the obvious limitations placed on her young life, Deirdre remains incredibly optimistic and upbeat and has discovered an inner strength she never knew she had. Much of this she attributes to the intercession of the Little Flower, herself all too familiar with bouts of illness and depression. 'I've already been to eight venues in Dublin,' she said enthusiastically, 'and I'll be going again. I just feel that Thérèse is so simple and special. And anything I have ever asked for, she has given to me.'

A Labour of Love

Pat Sweeney has been devoted to St Thérèse for many years. He and his wife Mary came to Lisieux for a holiday twenty years ago and immediately fell in love with Lisieux and with St Thérèse. Down the years, through his involvement with Fr Linus, Pat has got to know more and more about Thérèse and was very honoured when he was appointed manager and official driver of the Thérèsemobile. 'I feel very emotional about it,' Pat said, 'I can't imagine a greater privilege than that of driving the Relics of this great saint around Ireland.' Pat is a retired Regimental Sergeant-major and acknowledges that his army training was a great preparation for him to undertake the responsibility with confidence.

'I feel the great appeal of St Thérèse is her simplicity,' Pat said, 'She didn't complicate things. She herself loved God in a very simple way and all she wanted people to know was how much God loved them.' One of the things that pleased Pat most about the visit of St Thérèse was the fact that so many young people came to venerate the Relics. 'I have five daughters and four grandchildren,' Pat added, 'and I feel they will learn a lot from the visit of St Thérèse.'

Pat's co-driver, Jim Doyle, was equally proud of his part in this momentous event. 'I don't think the whole thing really dawned on me until it was all over,' he said, 'but it was a marvellous experience and one I will never forget.'

At Home with her Parents

It was on everybody's mind: images of the family-home in Alençon where she was born, and 'Les Buissonnets', the beautiful town-house in Lisieux where, in St Thérèse's own words, 'my life was truly happy'. Now she was coming home once again. This time to the newly dedicated Hospice – the first in Ireland to be named after her saintly parents, Louis and Zélie Martin. The Hospice in Blackrock, Co Dublin, is built on the site of the former Carmelite convent in Sweetman's Avenue and it was an emotional return for some of the members of that community who were there to welcome the Relics. Sr Mary (formerly Mother Teresa, Prioress of Blackrock) expressed the joy of all who were present: 'I see today as the beginning of a great work of care and service for the sick and elderly, inspired by the love and compassion which characterised the Martin family.'

The Reliquary then spent a few hours at Our Lady's Manor, Bullock Castle, Dalkey, run by the Carmelite sisters for the aged and infirm, bringing immense joy and happiness to the residents.

Visitor, Emma Lavin may be just seven years of age but she's a bit of an expert on St Thérèse. 'She was born in France and talked a funny language. Her mammy went to heaven when she was a baby so she played with her sisters instead. She was very holy and prayed a lot. She was always good and wore pretty dresses. She was sad sometimes but she talked to God and then everything would be okay.'

May 12

A Night to Remember

Late on Saturday night, the Relics of St Thérèse came to the Poor Clare convent in Ballsbridge. It was one of the most poignant moments in the nationwide tour of the 'Pilgrimage of Grace'. The Reliquary was carried by candlelight through the convent garden, passing the graves of the deceased

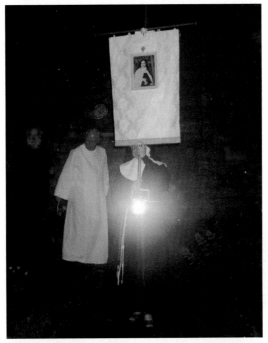

members of the community, who seemed to be present in the plaintive chant echoing around the cloisters. 'In a sense she is one of ourselves,' the Abbess remarked, 'and for us this is indeed a night to remember. St Thérèse, the great contemplative and woman of prayer,

has been a light for so many and she now comes to join her prayer to those of our own community for the salvation of the world.'

Sunday, 13 May was the feast of Our Lady of the Smile, the anniversary of the day St Thérèse was cured in 1883, a day when the community prayed in a special way to the Blessed Virgin – 'more Mother than Queen', as Thérèse wrote – for all who are sick, at home or in hospital.

Early on Sunday morning, the Reliquary was brought to the Church of St Thérèse in Mount Merrion, where a countless stream of parishioners came to welcome their Patroness and faithful Friend, to whom their church is proudly dedicated.

'She's got the biggest smile in heaven,' said Margaret Hoey, from inner-city Dublin. 'I queued for over two hours and was only in the church for a couple of minutes, but it felt a lot longer and it was well worth it. What this trip has done for our country we may never know.'

Festival of Choirs

The traffic on Dublin's Berkeley Road came to a standstill as the Thérèsemobile made its way to St Joseph's Carmelite Church. The Reliquary was carried shoulder-high along the street, flanked by a guard of honour and accompanied into the church by the haunting sound of bagpipes. Auxiliary Bishop of Dublin, Fiachra Ó Ceallaigh was there to welcome the Reliquary with the Carmelite community and crowds of parishioners. St Joseph's was a blaze of colour, with each of the ten shrines magnificently decorated, and pride of place given to the shrine of St Thérèse. A unique feature of the day was the presence of eight choirs who provided a feast of music and song right up to the midnight Mass. 'This is undoubtedly the most historic day in the history of our parish,' Parish Priest, Fr Patrick Keenan, OCD told the packed church, 'a day of grace and blessing that will never be forgotten.' Vivian Kavanagh, sacristan of St Joseph's for the past forty-five years, was equally impressed. 'I have never seen anything like it in all my years here,' he said, 'it has surpassed all our expectations.'

Throughout the day and all during the night, thousands of people came to venerate – with prayer, music and the perfumed scent of roses expressing the mood of the people and the spontaneous outpouring of joy and jubilation.

Local man, James Nolan acknowledged 'a deep sense of belonging' as he visited the Reliquary. 'I didn't really know what to expect,' he said honestly. 'It's very hard to explain, but you just feel it doesn't really matter who you are or what you have done, there is a sense of being welcomed. I think it is a marvellous event for the country and especially for the young.'

May 14 & 15

The People's Saint

The Church of Our Lady of Mount Carmel, Whitefriar Street, is one of the most historic and best-loved churches in Dublin city. The church, which had been specially painted and decorated for the occasion, proved to be a magnificent setting for the visit of the Relics of St Thérèse. It was by far the largest attendance that Whitefriar Street had ever seen, attracting an estimated crowd of over twenty-five thousand. It was also one of the most successful celebrations ever witnessed in the church. The response was overwhelming, with devotees arriving early to ensure their place. The Thérèsemobile was greeted by Fr Frank O'Gara, O Carm and the Carmelite community. Bishop Donal Lamont, O Carm, retired Bishop of Zimbabwe, was also present. On Monday there was a special Mass of Anointing for the sick at which Bishop Fiachra Ó Ceallaigh was the chief celebrant.

A notable feature of the visit was the continual flow of young people who attended the various ceremonies, while throughout the night quite a number of taxi-drivers kept dropping in for prayer. Overall, there was a wonderful sense of grace and blessing, and a spontaneous expression of joy and serenity pervaded the church.

Seventeen-year-old Kate and her friends, Tara and Louise, were on their way to a party when they 'came across' the crowds and decided to queue. 'I knew the Relics were in the city because my grandmother had told me about it,' Kate said. 'I didn't really plan to go and thought I might have to queue for hours, but I got in fairly quickly. I don't know much about Thérèse but I'll pray to her now to help me with my exams. There must be something special about her – why else would all these people be here?'

May 16

Everything is a Grace

'Everything is a grace' – even the rain! Such was the overall response to the visit of St Thérèse to the Carmelite convent, Firhouse. In fact, the 'soft Irish rain' seemed to add to the joy and enthusiasm of the historic event. 'I couldn't believe my eyes,' one woman said. 'At 11 o'clock at night, with the rain pouring down, there was a steady flow of people waiting to go in. No one seemed to mind. It did a lot for my own faith just to be there.' The small but beautiful chapel at Firhouse Carmel was a wonderful setting for Thérèse's final stop in Dublin before the Reliquary embarked on the remainder of the nation-wide tour. A bugle fanfare greeted the Thérèsemobile as it drove into the grounds, festooned with flags and bunting, plants and flowers. A large crowd had gathered with Bishop Eamonn Walsh, local priests, and the Carmelite friars and sisters to welcome the Relics. Children from the nearby Scoil Treasa and from the local Scouts formed a guard of honour. The Reliquary was carried through a magnificent rose-arch into the beautifully decorated chapel. The Reception Ceremony was joyous and festive, greatly enhanced by the music of the Garda Quintet, especially the haunting tones of a lone flautist during the reading of the psalm.

The Carmelite priests, together with the Dominican friars from Tallaght and Redemptorist sisters from Iona Road, joined the community and a full congregation in the joyful singing of Evening Prayer, led by the Firhouse parish choir. Huge numbers filed into the little chapel all day and well into the night, despite the low temperature and a few falls of snowflakes! The crowds were there again for Morning Prayer and a dawn Mass. It was lovely that the elderly and wheelchair-bound residents of the nearby Sally Park Nursing Home were also able to visit the Relics, thanks to the help of the students from Firhouse College.

It was indeed a gospel experience for one lady: 'St Thérèse wrote that only God knows the human heart. I was thinking the same thing myself as I watched people praying at the Reliquary. Some placed a rose on the glass; others touched it with their hands or rosary beads or with a prayer-card. It reminded me of the woman in the gospel who felt that if she could only touch the hem of Jesus' garment she would be healed.'

The Departure Ceremony, led by Bishop Donal Lamont, was especially moving. There was sadness and tears as the whole congregation waved farewell to the strains of *Time to Say Goodbye*. Thérèse herself seemed reluctant to leave as the Thérèsemobile moved slowly through the gates and off 'into the west'.

'My Name is Thérèse'

They were all there – Thérèse, Teresa, Treasa and Tess – sixty of them, each bearing the name of their patron saint. They proudly formed a guard of honour as the Thérèsemobile drew up to St James' Church, Athboy, chosen because of its past connection with the Carmelite Order. Today, the Church of Ireland bell-tower forms the only remaining building that marks the sixteenth-century Carmelite monastery.

Upwards of eight thousand pilgrims are estimated to have come for the afternoon visit of the Relics on the seventy-sixth anniversary of the canonisation of the Little Flower. The Reliquary was welcomed by Fr Patrick O'Connor, PP and borne into the church by an FCA guard of honour. There followed a three-hour period of veneration, during which time all who had waited patiently were able to file past the casket.

Margaret Mahon was there with her grandchildren, Stacey and Ciara, who at six years of age may have been a little too young to understand what was happening, but they were holding flowers and banners. 'Thérèse was a little girl and she had long, pretty hair,' said Stacey. 'My granny told me the story and everyone came today because she is on holiday in Ireland and she is very famous.' Margaret was equally impressed by the experience. 'I touched the casket with my rosary beads I've had for over forty years and felt a great peace. When the girls are older, I'll tell them they were here – it's something we will never see again.'

May 17

In the Heart of Ireland

From all across the midlands they came. Huge crowds lined the route into Mullingar and the streets and houses were decorated with statues and roadside shrines. The cortège slowly made its way through the town, accompanied by the local band, to the Cathedral of Christ the King, where Bishop Michael Smith was there to welcome the Reliquary.

'Thérèse had an extraordinary insight into her relationship with God, and to call her way "simple" may not be adequate,' Bishop Smith said. 'Her own faith was severely tested and the only thing that sustained her was her unwavering conviction of God's love for her.'

Children from the local schools visited with their teachers and there was a special evening Prayer Service for young adults. The nearby Hospitality Centre offered refreshments and displayed pictures and background information about Thérèse.

Fr Seán Henry, Administrator, was highly impressed by the great number of people who came, in particular the many parents who came with their families.

Alma Manny is a school teacher living in Mullingar and she was clearly animated following her visit to the cathedral. 'We're saying special prayers to St Thérèse at the moment for my five-year-old niece, Deirdre,' says Alma. 'Last year she was diagnosed with a rare neurological condition. She visited a convent and one of the nuns gave her a relic of St Thérèse and promised to pray for her. Deirdre returned to Dublin and her neurologist told the family that the results of the brain scan showed she did not have the genetic form as feared. Deirdre is very upbeat and positive,' smiled Alma, 'and today she wrote a prayer to St Thérèse, which she placed at the Reliquary.' With all the innocence and confidence of Thérèse herself, Alma said, 'This might just do it.'

Breaking Down Barriers

Following a successful novena of preparation, thousands of people gathered in St Mel's Cathedral to welcome the Relics of St Thérèse to their midland town of Longford. It could have been Croke Park on All Ireland Final Day as the crowds pushed excitedly towards the cathedral doors.

The Thérèsemobile made its way up the main street, to the sound of the Longford Pipe Band, flanked by members of the FCA. Bishop of Ardagh and Clonmacnois, Colm O'Reilly was there to receive the Reliquary, which was carried into the sanctuary by members of the pastoral council.

For Bishop Colm it was a unique occasion, and his deep-felt joy was evident as he spoke. 'I'm a late convert to St Thérèse,' he admitted. 'When I was very young I always thought she wasn't a "man's saint"; then I read *Story of a Soul* and discovered the real St Thérèse. The true human person began to emerge and I realised that there was a much greater depth of spirituality to her than I ever imagined. Some people may feel that because of their own particular lifestyle they have no place here today, but that is to miss the whole purpose of her visit. Everyone here is welcome and Thérèse has broken down the barriers. Her presence here today has opened up the love of God to everyone and that is what we need to see.'

One of the real surprises of the visit was the amount of people who gathered for the early morning Mass. 'We certainly didn't expect the cathedral to be full for the dawn Mass, but it was, and it proved a wonderful finish to the all-night Vigil,' said Fr Vincent Connaughton.

As the Reliquary left, the mood of celebration remained, with the novena continuing over the weekend.

James Cox was in Longford and was amazed at the crowds. 'I've been to all the preparatory talks in the cathedral over the past week. I was really impressed with Bishop Brendan Comiskey and with John Lonergan, Governor of Mountjoy Prison. It was a whole week of celebration and today is the highlight. I think Thérèse herself would be very happy to have received such a warm welcome.'

May 19

Blessing and Anointing

The Reliquary was led through the streets of Moate by a procession headed by two pipers, a colour party of scouts, school children and altar servers. On the way, the procession stopped for a moment of prayer at the Church of Ireland and at St Patrick's Parish Church. Fr Bernard O'Reilly, O Carm, Prior, Fr Michael Walsh, PP and the Carmelite community were waiting at the priory church door to recite the prayers of welcome before the Relics were carried into the tastefully decorated church by members of the Military Police and the FCA bearer party, accompanied by First Communion children. Pupils from the Convent of Mercy National School sang for the opening service, and students from Moate Community School led the readings and prayers. Veneration of the Relics continued non-stop, day and night. Many invalids and people in wheelchairs came, and Anointing of the Sick was provided throughout the duration of the visit. A specially constructed wheelchair-friendly confessional was also available. Nine Masses took place during the twenty-two-hour visit, six indoors and three outdoors on the tennis courts, for which the Moate Variety Group and the local folk group provided the music. Carmel Boyle sang at various intervals from her popular album, *White Wings and Roses*, based on the poetry of St Thérèse. Harpist, Mary Kelly also performed during the ceremonies and Dancezone presented a beautiful mime in honour of St Thérèse.

All who helped were delighted with the response, especially 'with the thousands of people with disabilities and serious illnesses who visited the Reliquary. Seeing their faith and watching them pray moved many of the stewards to tears again and again.' Fr Bernard also said that one of the most moving incidents of the weekend occurred as the Reliquary was leaving Moate. A man brought his wheelchair-bound son to the Thérèsemobile and two helpers lifted up the wheelchair so that the boy could touch the casket. 'This,' he added, 'typified the spirit of the visit.'

A Link with Lisieux

Brilliant summer weather blessed the visit of St Thérèse's Relics to the motherhouse of the Medical Missionaries of Mary in Drogheda. From mid-afternoon on Sunday, 20 May, people of all ages came to pray and lay their petitions before St Thérèse. Many organisations

from the town joined with the sisters in preparing for this very special event. Ambulances ferried in many people from out of town, while forty wheelchairs brought patients from the nearby Lourdes Hospital and devoted staff accompanied another fifty patients coming on foot, some even with drips or in plaster casts.

Large numbers remained in the auditorium throughout the all-night Vigil and it was packed to capacity for the morning Mass celebrated by Archbishop Seán Brady. Chaplain, Fr Paddy Rushe admitted to being 'quite stunned' by the lengthy queues of people and the display of public warmth. 'I think Irish Society is not anti-God, but the Celtic Tiger has left a huge gap in society. I see it in

the people who come here to the hospital. Many feel empty and lost. Many have childhood memories of Thérèse, and her visit renews their sense of faith and trust in God.'

As the Thérèsemobile was leaving, it paused at the entrance to the hospital in which a brick from the infirmary where St Thérèse died is embedded in the altar; it is just opposite the cemetery where Mother Mary Martin, foundress of the Medical Missionaries, is buried.

Sr Isabelle took up the story: 'Our foundress had great devotion to St Thérèse. In 1947, she went to Lisieux where she met Thérèse's sister, Mother Agnès (Pauline) and told her about her difficulties and struggles in those early years of the Congregation. Mother Agnès gave her a brick from the infirmary where Thérèse died and this precious gift is now located in the hospital chapel.'

The community and the local parish choir joined in the singing of the *Regina Coeli* as they reluctantly waved goodbye to St Thérèse.

May 21

A Saint for our Times

People from all parts of the Diocese of Kilmore converged on the county's capital for the visit of the Reliquary of St Thérèse of Lisieux. It was a unique opportunity for people to be in the presence of this famous saint. A lone piper accompanied the Reliquary as it was carried by members of the FCA from O'Neill Barracks to the Cathedral of St Patrick and St Felim – blessed, in 1938, on the feast-day of St Thérèse – where it was received by Bishop Leo O'Reilly.

'The coming of St Thérèse is a time for prayer, reflection and listening to the word of God,' Bishop Leo said, as he warmly welcomed all who gathered in the cathedral. Later, at the midnight Mass, he referred to St Thérèse as 'a saint for our times', whose whole life was motivated by love. Her 'Little Way' anticipated the teaching of the Second Vatican Council that all God's people are called to a life of holiness.

A poignant incident took place as the Thérèsemobile was leaving Cavan town. Driver Pat Sweeney related the story: 'At the request of one of the Gardaí escorting us, we stopped to say a prayer at a little archway in the centre of the town, where a popular Cavan man, Paddy Jackson, had been killed a few days earlier. As we continued on our way, we came to Ballinagh, where a crowd had gathered outside the church. It was in fact Paddy Jackson's funeral. The family was amazed to see that the Reliquary had stopped outside the church, as they had been unable to visit the cathedral because of the funeral. We immediately opened the back of the Thérèsemobile for them, and Paddy's widow and family were able to spend some time in prayer beside the Relics. It was a heart-rending scene but at the same time a moment of grace for the family, one Thérèse had obviously planned, to comfort the family in their terrible loss.'

The Abbey *en fête*

The Norbertine Order has a special link with St Thérèse, as Fr Godefroid Madelaine, Prior of Mondaye Abbey near Lisieux, was the first to read through and approve Thérèse's manuscript in 1898. He was also the one who suggested the title, *Story of a Soul*, by which the autobiography is still known today.

The exquisite grounds of Kilnacrott Abbey, Ballyjamesduff, home to the Norbertine Order in Ireland, was a perfect setting for the visit of St Thérèse, and the abbey grounds were packed day and night with countless pilgrims from far and wide. The sun shone brilliantly on the assembled crowds, and a dazzling display of flowers, decorations and side-altars contributed to the atmosphere of prayer and joy. Fr Gerry Cusack, Prior, and the Norbertine community received the Reliquary at the gates of the abbey.

With the blessing of idyllic weather, the community decided to have the evening Mass in the open air. A huge crowd, from all over the county, spread out across the abbey grounds. The chief celebrant was Fr Gerry Cusack. In the homily, Fr Eugene McCaffrey, one of the visiting Carmelites, spoke of the message of God's merciful love and forgiveness as Thérèse herself had discovered it in the gospel.

The visit, however, was a bitter-sweet occasion for the abbey. Popular member of the community, Fr Martin Kenny, who had a life-long devotion to the saint, passed away during the visit. 'When Thérèse left,' Fr Gerry said, 'she took Fr Martin home.'

May 23

Hope for Cooley

The people of the Cooley Peninsula and the surrounding area of approximately six hundred homes had been devastated by the recent foot and mouth epidemic which wiped out livelihoods and caused such hardship to the families.

Fr Linus Ryan believed that it was important to visit the area. 'We knew that families had been absolutely devastated, not just financially, but their whole way of life had disappeared. You can still see the suffering: wild flowers are growing where there are no sheep grazing. So we wanted to visit as an act of solidarity.' Parish Priest, Fr Peter McParland spoke eloquently of the joy and hope that the visit meant to the local community.

On Sunday, 20 May, in Newry Cathedral, the pupils from the Sacred Heart Grammar School presented a delightful performance of The Arms of Jesus – A Conversation with Thérèse of Lisieux. *The play, written and produced by Brenda Rankin, Head of Drama, is built around a conversation between Thérèse and two sixth-year students. Mime and tableaux are used to reinforce the words of the saint.*

Heaven Knows no Frontiers

Any suggestion that the response would be diminished in any way when the pilgrimage crossed the border was completely dispelled as soon as the Thérèsemobile reached the first stop, in Newry town. Tens of thousands of people came from all over Northern Ireland during the eight-day visit. There was a high level of coverage on television and radio, and in the local newspapers. 'The miracle,' one reporter said, 'was not the numbers, but the fact that the Reliquary spent eight days in the North without incident.' At every venue, the Reliquary was received and escorted with great courtesy by the RUC.

A lone piper flanked the cortège as the Relics of St Thérèse made their way to the Cathedral of SS Patrick and Colman, where Bishop of Dromore, John McAreavey, alongside retired Bishop Francis Gerard Brooks, received the Reliquary in the presence of a large crowd. Following a short Ceremony of Welcome, veneration began, and there was an air of

Thérèse under the Stars

quiet celebration and joy in the busy north-ern town as residents and shopkeepers came out onto the streets to catch a glimpse of this historic coming. As the Relics entered the cathedral, they were accompanied by a delightful liturgical dance-musical performed by local school children.

In his address of welcome, Bishop McAreavey told the congregation that his deepest hope and prayer on this special day was 'that Thérèse's visit will help the people of Newry and of the diocese to appreciate more fully the divine life that surrounds us and renew in our hearts a deeper awareness of the love of God that we have received.' For the rest of the day, the crowds visiting the Relics were continuous, with the queues at times stretch-ing along several streets, both in front of and behind the cathedral. Throughout the vener-ation, extracts from the writings of St Thérèse were read aloud. The visit to Newry came to an end all too quickly, but Thérèse had an appointment with her Carmelite sisters in nearby Glenvale, a few miles outside the town.

The stars shone brightly in the night sky as the Relics of St Thérèse arrived at the beauti-fully situated Carmelite convent in Glenvale, on the outskirts of Newry. Did Thérèse her-self look up and see a large 'T' in the night sky and remember her prophetic words as a child, the evening she walked home with her father, 'My name is written in heaven'? It was certainly written in the hearts of all who waited in the gathering darkness for that 'never-to-be-forgotten' night visit to Glenvale. It was a magnificent sight, as the hundreds of people, with candles flickering in the twi-light, escorted the Thérèsemobile along the route. There was an unmitigated sense of joy and celebration; the grounds swarmed with children, parents with babies in arms and delighted friends and associates of the Carmelite sisters. Bishop Francis Gerard Brooks, retired Bishop of Dromore, was there with Fr Francis Boyle, Parish Priest of Saval, to recite the opening prayers. Members of the local Saval GAA club carried the cas-ket into the festively decorated chapel. Sr Teresa Margaret gave a moving address of welcome. She recalled some of the historic events associated with Glenvale since the coming of the Carmelites in 1929 and thanked the people of the locality for their continual support over the years. Veneration continued all night. The chapel was never empty right up to midday when an all-too-short visit came to an end.

May 24

Dancing at Lurgan

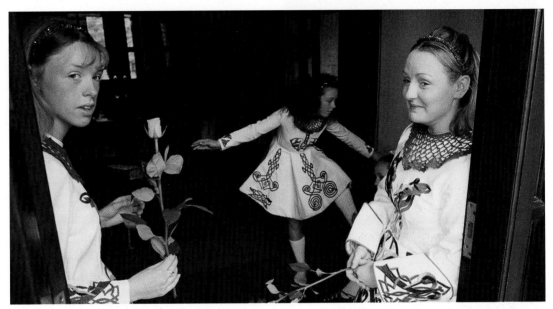

Irish dancers and school children from the parish provided a guard of honour as St Thérèse arrived at St Peter's Church, Shankill, Lurgan. The Reliquary was greeted by Dean Arthur Byrne and carried into the church by members of local GAA clubs.

Fr Terence Rafferty treated the congregation to a magnificent organ-recital as the Reliquary was carried into the sanctuary. Veneration continued all day and was followed by a Night Vigil, which ended with an early morning Mass. The chief celebrant, Fr John Byrne, expressed the gratitude of all the people of Lurgan who had experienced the joy and blessing of this unique occasion. A notable feature of the visit was the number of non-Catholics who were in evidence at the event.

'I just can't believe the crowds,' said tourist, Bernard O'Hara who was born in New York but has Irish blood running through his veins. 'My mother came from Donegal and this is my first time here for over thirty years. It's incredible to see so many people coming together, all the flowers and altars. It's something I never thought I'd see, something I thought was gone forever.' He added, 'I've taken loads of pictures to show the people back home, and it's really special to be here at this time because I don't think it will happen again in my lifetime.'

Shower of Roses

The famous carillon bells of St Patrick's Cathedral, Armagh, the ecclesiastical capital of Ireland, rang out joyously as the Relics of St Thérèse were carried by members of the Order of Malta to the cathedral door, to be greeted by Auxiliary Bishop of Armagh, Gerard Clifford. Even as he spoke, thousands of people gasped in awe as rose petals showered down from the twin spires of the cathedral onto the casket of the 'Little

May 25

Flower'. It was a beautiful moment of joy and celebration for all who witnessed it. Children from St Catherine's Primary School sang *Set Your Hearts on the Higher Gifts* during the Welcoming Ceremony.

The cathedral was packed for the midnight Mass celebrated by Bishop Clifford. He said: 'I think the whole prayerful atmosphere of the visit is an expression of the love of the people of Armagh archdiocese for Thérèse. The attitude of quiet, gentle prayerfulness tells its own story. This is a very special moment in our lives, particularly for those who have come with sick people or with their own cares and worries. I have every confidence that they will be supported and encouraged by Thérèse's presence here today. She is telling us what spirituality is all about: doing our own work with joy and doing it very well, extraordinarily well – that's her message.'

Helen McDaid was there to venerate the Relics. 'I have great devotion to St Thérèse because back in 1992 I got cancer. I did a novena to her and have had many signs of her help since. Ask, and she will send you a rose. I have had three roses from her: a red rose in 1992, a white rose three years ago and a yellow rose in Lourdes last year. We are very privileged to have her here today; it's not every day a saint comes to visit.'

A Distinguished Guest

St Macartan's Cathedral, Monaghan, was packed to capacity hours before the Reliquary arrived. A large crowd had already gathered to meet the Thérèsemobile at the town's Old Cross, from where it made its way to the cathedral, escorted by members of the FCA and headed by Monaghan Community Brass Band. Homes and shops throughout the town were colourfully decorated with altars, portraits of the saint and bright floral bouquets. Children from the local schools scattered rose petals along the route. Fr Pádraig McKenna and representatives of the local and diocesan clergy were on hand to receive the Reliquary. Throughout the whole visit, a guard of honour was provided by the primary and secondary school children from the town and by local boy scouts and girl guides. There was a constant flow of visitors throughout the night; many people spent the entire night in the presence of the Relics. The Saturday vigil Mass and all

the Sunday Masses were packed to capacity. The presence of Thérèse, who so loved the Eucharist, added a special atmosphere to the liturgical celebrations. The Bishop of Clogher, Joseph Duffy, officiated at the Liturgy of Departure on Sunday morning as the people of Monaghan bade farewell to their distinguished guest. From there, the Thérèsemobile once again crossed over the border on its way to Belfast.

May 27-29

Thérèse the Peacemaker

It is estimated that over 120,000 people venerated the Relics of St Thérèse during the three-day visit to Belfast. Crowds of people travelled from as far away as Glasgow to take part in this historic event. Many of the Protestant community also came and joined in the celebrations.

West Belfast witnessed amazing scenes as the Relics of St Thérèse arrived at St Peter's Cathedral on the Falls Road. First Communion children formed a guard of honour around the casket, which was carried to the steps of the cathedral by members of the local GAA Dwyer's Club. Bishop of Down and Connor, Patrick Walsh received the Reliquary at the cathedral door. Speaking at the Opening Ceremony, he welcomed St Thérèse to Belfast on the feast of the Ascension and drew parallels between her personal suffering and that of the local community down through the years. 'The attraction cannot be solely the ornate casket or even the bones of the saint,' he said. 'The attraction must be the saint herself – and her message: a message of love, one that appeals to the deeper and more spiritual part of our human nature.'

The clergy and religious of the diocese gathered in St Peter's for Evening Prayer, wishing to mark the presence of the saint by a service of renewal and commitment to their own calling. Confessions continued for nineteen hours of the twenty-two-hour visit, as huge numbers of people availed of the opportunity to celebrate the Sacrament of Reconciliation. Several services took place on Monday morning, especially for the children of the parish, including a concelebrated Mass, at which Cardinal Daly spoke passionately of the significance of St Thérèse's visit for the city of Belfast and for the whole country.

The following day, after a brief Farewell Ceremony conducted by Auxiliary Bishop of Down and Connor, Donal McKeown, the Thérèsemobile left St Peter's and travelled along the Falls Road, close to the peace line, to nearby Clonard Monastery. Though it was only a short distance, the procession had to make its way slowly through the enthusiastic crowds of people that lined the route. Fr Brendan O'Rourke and the Redemptorist community were on hand to welcome St Thérèse. A Triduum in honour of the Little Flower had already taken place in Clonard in preparation for the Belfast visit. The Reliquary was carried into the sanctuary by members of the community, to a powerful organ improvisation of the *Gregorian Alleluia*.

Scenes similar to those witnessed in St Peter's took place once again as crowds of people came day and night to venerate the Relics.

The next day, the Reliquary made its way slowly to the Holy Cross Passionist Church, Ardoyne. On the way, there was a two-hour stop at St Paul's Church on the Falls Road, where a special service of Anointing of the Sick took place. The procession continued along the Falls Road, through the New Lodge area and into Cliftonville Road, for a twenty-minute stopover at the Poor Clare convent. The short distance from Clonard to Ardoyne took over two hours to cover, such was the extraordinary outpouring of devotion as masses of people crowded the route,

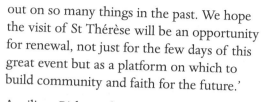

May 27-29

and school children formed a guard of honour along the way. Streets and homes that had experienced so much pain and suffering in recent years were ablaze with bunting, flags, roadside altars and banners saying: 'Welcome, St Thérèse.' In what was seen as an historic development, Holy Cross Church was able to remain open all night for the first time in thirty years. The significance of the day was not lost on the clergy who had been involved in its preparation. 'This area,' said Fr Gary Donegan, CP, 'has missed out on so many things in the past. We hope the visit of St Thérèse will be an opportunity for renewal, not just for the few days of this great event but as a platform on which to build community and faith for the future.'

Auxiliary Bishop of Down and Connor, Anthony Farquhar led the Prayers of Farewell, as the Reliquary left Ardoyne for Derry.

Fr Linus Ryan was particularly touched with the atmosphere in the Northern Ireland venues. 'It has been an unbelievable experience,' he said, 'after thirty years of violence, suffering and strife, to see people coming to church to celebrate, rather than for a funeral or some sad occasion. After the troubles, people are learning to love again. We hope that Thérèse will help finish what has been started so well by the peace process.'

Peggy McKee from Belfast came with her granddaughter, Stacey. 'Stacey is only three so she's a bit too young to understand what is really happening,' said the proud grandmother, 'but I'll tell her all about it one day. St Thérèse was always a part of our family and both my parents had a strong devotion to her. I've prayed to her many times and have often thought about going on a pilgrimage to Lisieux, but her coming to Ireland is even better. It's more personal and especially nice when you're in your own home town with your family and friends around you.'

'A Rose for Peace'

For a community which has felt tremendous pain and suffered such loss of life down through the years, it was refreshing to see the people of Derry united in an experience of joy in the presence of the Lord. Thérèse was the one who brought them together in St Eugene's Cathedral.

Traffic was brought to a complete standstill as tens of thousands of people lined the road from Dungiven to Derry. The procession to the cathedral made an impressive sight as young and old, clutching 'a rose for peace', followed the Thérèsemobile in reverent silence across the Foyle Bridge and along Culmore Road, slowly making its way to St Eugene's. As the cathedral bells began to chime, the Knights of Malta, the Red Cross and the St John's Ambulance carried the casket into the sanctuary where it was greeted by Bishop of Derry, Séamus Hegarty and Auxiliary Bishop, Francis Lagan. Bishop Hegarty celebrated a special Mass in the packed cathedral that evening while thousands huddled outside in the rain, awaiting their turn to venerate.

Bishop Hegarty was enthusiastic about the public response. 'The people of Derry are good people and they are not missing this opportunity. They are patiently queuing in colossal numbers and it is certainly reassuring for me as bishop. There are those who say the faith is dead. The faith is not dead by any means; it is very strong and evident. It is a matter of giving people an opportunity to participate more fully in the life of the church. People cannot be forced or coerced, but I have no doubt that this is a time of grace, a very special occasion indeed. This is simply profound.'

For BBC broadcaster and television presenter, Gerry Anderson, the visit of the Relics of St Thérèse and the reaction it generated in 'Stroke City' was a curious and intriguing one. While driving round his home town, the Derry man identified modern buildings and isolated sites where once there were treasured memories and sentimental journeys of years past – now callously obliterated with the onset of the troubles. 'There is nothing left to remind me of my child-hood,' he said mournfully. 'Yet walking in the midst of the animated people within the grounds of St Eugene's Cathedral is a bit like coming home. I used to sing here as a choirboy and it really brings me back to my childhood. I've often wondered what had happened to the people who came, and it's great to see them all here again.'

May 31

Thérèse by Candlelight

The Carmelite Retreat Centre, Termonbacca, nestling at the foot of the Bogside, was a buzz of excitement and anticipation as the Thérèsemobile made its way up the steep hill lined with school children. The Relics were received by Fr Seán Conlon, OCD and the Carmelite community. The Reliquary was placed in the recently-built lecture hall, beautifully adorned with masses of floral bouquets and pictures of St Thérèse.

A stream of visitors came all day and throughout the night. All roads leading to the monastery were continuously lined with traffic travelling to and fro. Many people were delighted to join the community in the celebration of Evening and Morning Prayer of the Church and, for most, the candlelight Mass in the early hours of the morning was undoubtedly the highlight of the Night Vigil.

Bishop Séamus Hegarty was present for the final concelebrated Mass the following morning, to escort Thérèse on her way across the border to Co Donegal.

Fr Seán was overwhelmed by the incredible turnout. He has always had a great devotion to the Little Flower, dating back to early childhood, and it has grown deeper over the years. 'I feel a great sense of community here today, people have been coming all during the night. I see a deep hunger and a sense of occasion, even more so than at Christmas or Easter. Today is a sign of providence, a sign that God's grace is at work. Thérèse promised she would do good on earth. I never thought I'd see the day when she would fulfil this promise so literally, here in Derry.'

Margaret Peoples and her daughter, Catherine, were privileged to be part of the guard of honour in Termonbacca. For Margaret in particular, it is a day she will never forget. 'Some years ago, Thérèse sent me a rose. At the time, I was really troubled and asked her to send me a sign. I had been praying very hard about it and when my brother got married two months later, I was given a beautiful red rose. It was only the next day that I realised this was Thérèse's way of saying that everything was well.'

Double Celebration

Raphoe was always guaranteed to attract huge crowds of people coming to welcome the Relics of the Little Flower. Bishop of Raphoe, Philip Boyce met the Thérèsemobile at the Derry-Donegal border. A large crowd had gathered at the Station Roundabout to escort the Reliquary to the Cathedral of St Eunan and St Columba. Fr Eamonn Kelly welcomed Thérèse on behalf of the people of the diocese and reminded them that the visit coincided with the one hundredth anniversary of the consecration of the cathedral in June, 1901. The visit of St Thérèse was a fitting start to these celebrations.

To commemorate the historic event, Bishop Boyce wrote a Pastoral Letter which was distributed to all homes throughout the diocese. Despite the inclement weather, crowds of people continued to visit throughout the night and again the following morning. At midnight, the spirals of people, young and old, stretched from the entrance of Lower Ard O'Donnell to the cathedral door as the crowd continued to swell, waiting to venerate the Relics of the saint.

For Bishop Philip Boyce, himself a Carmelite like St Thérèse, it was a particularly moving experience. He was ordained bishop on the feast-day of the Little Flower. 'She is a saint for the ordinary people,' he said affectionately. 'People are able to grasp the meaning of her "Little Way". They do not see it as something beyond them. Thérèse is a reminder to all of us that holiness is not complicated or extraordinary. People are coming, not just out of curiosity, but because there is a real hunger for God, for spirituality and for truth. And Thérèse's message is meeting that need.'

The following morning, Fr Eamonn Kelly celebrated a farewell Mass, with Donegal-born Carmelite, Fr Frank Gallagher as guest preacher.

Veronica McGowan described the experience as 'the realisation of a dream'. 'I've had a great devotion to the Little Flower all my life and she has never let me down. But I would never be able to afford to go and see her home town of Lisieux. This visit has been great for the country because it gives everyone an opportunity to honour her.'

June 2

Young Carmelites in Waiting

Banners, bunting, flags and roadside shrines lined the road as the Thérèsemobile arrived in the picturesque seaside town of Falcarragh in the very heart of the Donegal Gaeltacht. There was a wonderful sense of occasion and a hearty 'Céad Míle Fáilte' for the Little Flower as Fr Con Cunningham, PP welcomed the Relics and led the procession through the small village, accompanied by the local Céilí band and a group of little girls dressed as Carmelite nuns! The guard of honour consisted of children from the local football team, together with a line of Donegal women, all of whom had been christened Thérèse.

A wonderful community spirit pervaded the entire visit and a warm greeting was given in three languages: Irish, English, and French in honour of the country in which Thérèse was born. Veneration continued throughout the day and night, and the beautiful church of Falcarragh was filled to capacity for the vigil Mass of Pentecost Sunday. Prayers and readings continued all night. For many people, a special feature was the presence of Daniel O'Donnell, who came with the parishioners of Kincasslagh and led the congregation in singing hymns. Following the 11 o'clock Mass on Sunday morning, the local Céilí band, accompanied once again by the 'Carmelite nuns', escorted Thérèse onwards to her next destination.

A Time of Grace

At every venue, confessors were available to administer the Sacrament of Reconciliation. For those involved it was a moving experience, as literally thousands availed of the opportunity, often well into the early hours of the morning. 'These were "mission confessions",' said Fr Des Flanagan, O Carm, one of the official chaplains to the tour. 'It was like a Christmas Eve rush all day long.' Certainly it was a time of grace and healing for many people who took St Thérèse at her word and accepted the message of God's forgiveness and mercy.

June 3

A Pentecost Celebration

It was little wonder that Thérèse was somewhat late for her appointment with the people of the lovely village of Bruckless. All along the way, through the hills of Donegal, the Thérèsemobile was literally 'hijacked' by enthusiastic groups which had gathered near homes and roadside shrines, adorned with flowers and pictures of the saint.

The Reliquary was greeted by the Ardaghey Pipe Band and led to the church by the First Communion girls, who scattered roses along the route. The fact that it was Pentecost Sunday added to the spirit of joy and festivity. Fr Dermot McShane, PP, together with Mgr Andrew Carrabin, the oldest priest in the Raphoe Diocese, conducted the Ceremony of Welcome, and the Reliquary was carried into the church of SS Joseph and Conal to the strains of *Faith of our Fathers*.

Fr McShane, who visits Lisieux each year, said it was 'a proud moment for the parish and one that would give fresh confidence to the local community', but he also acknowledged the note of sadness in the parish because of the sudden death, two weeks previously, of retired Garda, John Feeney, who was the principal coordinator of the Bruckless visit.

As someone well known for drawing spectacular crowds, it seemed strange to see Daniel O'Donnell playing second fiddle for once! But play it he did as Thérèse stole the limelight, and rightly so, according to Ireland's own Northern Star, who described his visit to Falcarragh as 'a privilege and an honour'. 'It is almost incredible,' he added, 'how this young woman could create such an extraordinary response and bring so many people together in west Donegal.'

Thirteen-year-old Sinéad Cronin had already visited the Reliquary the day before in Falcarragh, but wanted to go again. 'I was there last night and it was really peaceful and intimate. My friends came here with me today and we got some roses blessed. Thérèse wasn't much older than any of us, so we feel close to her. I'll probably read her book after this. She lets you see God as a friend, not a distant figure.'

Thérèse's Radioman

From Mountjoy to Mullingar, Longford to Lough Derg, Belfast to Bruckless, he was there, complete with microphone and dictaphone, the man who expertly delivered Thérèse's message to those who could not be present at every venue. RTÉ broadcaster Donncha Ó Dúlaing first referred to St Thérèse at the beginning of the nationwide tour on Easter Sunday, and from that moment on, the story took on a life of its own. So taken was Donncha by the scenes he witnessed and the people he met, that he set off on the 'Thérèse Trail', which became a series of updates on the tour via his Saturday night programme, *Fáilte Isteach*. For weeks he spoke to men, women and children and gathered personal stories and testimonies in his own inimitable style before broadcasting them over the airwaves to his many listeners, both at home and abroad. The Cork man unintentionally fell into the role of messenger and became our affable travelling companion throughout our journey – and for the popular broadcaster it was an experience he will never forget.

June 4

Thérèse in the Yeats County

Thousands of people turned out on the June Bank Holiday for the visit of the Relics of St Thérèse to the Yeats County. *En route* for the town, the Reliquary visited St Thérèse's Church in Ballintogher, Co Sligo, where it was received by Bishop of Ardagh and Clonmacnois, Colm O'Reilly. The church is one of the few in the country to have relics of the French saint. During the two-hour visit, over two thousand people visited the church to venerate the Relics.

The First Communion children, local scouts and girl guides, members of the FCA and the Knights of St Columbanus escorted the Relics into the sanctuary. There was an almost mystical atmosphere in the cathedral: clouds of incense filled the air and hundreds of candles flickered in and around the sanctuary. In front of the altar stood a beautifully illuminated 'Tree of Life', colourfully decorated with pictures of St Thérèse. The cathedral holds about eight hundred people and was full throughout the visit. Veneration continued all through the night, with queues extending round the cathedral most of the time.

The presence of most of the diocesan clergy, who were on their annual retreat in Sligo, added to the solemnity of the farewell Mass on Tuesday morning, celebrated by Bishop Christopher Jones.

In Sligo, the Reliquary was received by Bishop of Elphin, Christopher Jones, together with priests and religious from the diocese.

Martin McCabe was among the many visitors to the cathedral. 'I had already visited the Relics when they were in Dublin and found the whole experience very peaceful and emotional. I wouldn't consider myself particularly religious but it was nice to get away from the hustle and bustle of city life and have a bit of quiet time for myself. I don't know much about St Thérèse but I have been following the tour since day one and I am certainly very interested in her now!'

A Treasured Souvenir

A festive atmosphere surrounded St Muredach's Cathedral, Ballina, in the Diocese of Killala, for the arrival of the Relics of St Thérèse. Though overcast skies threatened rain, the good weather held until later in the evening. Members of the local FCA provided a guard of honour, and the First Communion classes of boys and girls scattered rose petals as the Thérèsemobile came into the cathedral grounds. Bishop Thomas Finnegan welcomed the Relics with a short Prayer Ceremony at the door of the cathedral before members of the Lions Club carried the Reliquary into the sanctuary.

Bishop Finnegan had published a commemorative booklet for the occasion, entitled *The Greatest Saint of Modern Times*, which was distributed throughout the diocese and will be kept as a treasured souvenir of St Thérèse's visit. 'I hope the booklet,' he said, 'will be a keepsake of a momentous occasion for our diocese and a continuous reminder, for all, of the teaching and message of St Thérèse.'

Despite the onset of late-night rain, crowds continued to visit the cathedral into the early hours of the morning.

Sheila McKay was at St Muredach's. 'My sister, Rose, was very ill some years ago and we asked St Thérèse to intercede on her behalf. Rose came through her illness and we certainly attribute her recovery to St Thérèse. She now lives in England and would love to have been here herself. Instead, I'm getting a rose blessed and am bringing it back for her. I don't know what the secret of Thérèse's appeal is but if you could bottle it, you'd make a fortune!'

June 6

A Time of Renewal

The heavy rain did not deter the large crowds who came to the Cathedral of the Annunciation and St Nathy, Ballaghaderreen, the only Co Roscommon venue to feature in the nationwide tour of the Relics of St Thérèse of Lisieux. Bishop of Achonry, Thomas Flynn received the Reliquary at the cathedral door and Boyle FCA with representatives from local groups provided a guard of honour. Children scattered rose petals and sang hymns of welcome as the casket was placed in front of the altar. People of all ages came throughout the night to pray and spend time with the Little Flower. Parishes in the diocese took responsibility for various times of veneration. It was moving to see so many sick people, and people in wheelchairs, who were given priority at all times in approaching the Reliquary. The cathedral was packed for Evening Prayer and for the evening Mass, celebrated by Bishop Flynn. 'It was certainly a time of grace and of great spiritual renewal for the parish,' said Fr Michael Reilly, Administrator.

A Legion of Helpers

St Thérèse's prayer for a 'legion of little souls' was answered to the letter by an army of helpers, volunteers, caterers, stewards and car park attendants at every venue throughout the land, who offered their services willingly and generously both in the weeks leading up to the visit and on the day itself. Local committees worked non-stop, often to the point of exhaustion, to make the visit a success. Most venues had anything from two to four hundred volunteers, which meant a huge number of people were part of making the 'Pilgrimage of Grace' one of the greatest religious events ever experienced in the country. God loves the cheerful giver, and it was joy and cheerfulness that most characterised what was essentially 'a labour of love' for all involved.

June 7

Grace-Filled Moment

It was a cold, windy afternoon for those waiting at the Cathedral of the Assumption, Tuam, for the visit of St Thérèse. Yet the crowds were in no way deterred, for the cathedral itself and its grounds were packed as the Thérèsemobile arrived. Members of Boyle FCA carried the Reliquary to the cathedral door. As Archbishop Michael Neary gave thanks 'for this grace-filled moment', the Tuam Brass Band played hymns of welcome, and First Communion children formed a guard of honour. Despite the rain, thousands of people came to venerate the Relics, many waiting patiently and with great dignity for their own time with the Little Flower in the beautifully decorated cathedral.

The Blessing of Roses took place every hour for the duration of the visit, and a special souvenir booklet was made available. In a marquee erected near the cathedral for the occasion, a catering committee supplied refreshments for visitors, many of whom commented, 'It was wonderful to see so many people of all ages "connecting with God" through St Thérèse.'

At the evening Mass, Archbishop Neary spoke of the significance of the visit of St Thérèse as 'a very special moment of grace and renewal for the archdiocese'. The music for the Mass, provided by the excellent cathedral choir, made the occasion one of special joy and celebration. During the Night Vigil, thousands venerated the Relics with great reverence and prayerfulness. The Relics left on Friday morning for Knock, following a farewell Mass.

Just before the Relics left, Eileen came for her second visit, this time to give thanks. Her teenage son, David, had been suffering from depression for the past six months. He had dropped out of school, cut himself off from his friends and spent most of the time in his room. Eileen had asked him to come with her to visit the Reliquary but he refused. However, later that night he left the house on his own and went to the cathedral. He came home late and went to his room without saying a word. Next morning, his parents were amazed to see David in the kitchen, dressed in his school uniform and carrying books under his arm, ready for school. 'Thérèse, who hated school so much and had so many dark moments herself, seems to have in some way connected with David and given him new hope for the future. Certainly, for our family the visit of Thérèse has brought a joy and blessing we did not expect.'

June 8

'Like Mother, like Daughter'

'Like mother, like daughter' they say, and so it proved to be at Tranquilla Carmelite convent. Just as it had been raining when Our Lady appeared at the gable wall in Knock, so a gentle rain was falling as the Relics of St Thérèse, led by a colour party of the FCA, arrived at the convent, where they were welcomed by Archbishop Michael Neary of Tuam, Fr Liam Finnerty, OCD, the community and a large gathering of people. 'Fáilte rómhat, a Threasa óig, Fáilte rómhat, a Threasa óig, céad fáilte chuig Tranquilla' greeted her in song as the Reliquary drew up. The skies cleared and brightened, and the Welcoming Ceremony began in the open air, while First Communion children scattered red rose petals.

Veneration of the Relics continued for a full twenty-two hours, in a calm and beautiful atmosphere. People sat quietly in the chapel and choir, soaking up an indefinable sense of joy, love and togetherness – it was an experience of the sacred and of being with God. The Benedictine sisters from Kylemore Abbey joined the community for sung Vespers of St Thérèse, for Night Prayer and for Morning Prayer. The Night Vigil passed in silence and prayer, with occasional readings from the writings of St Thérèse, songs from

June 9 & 10

At Our Lady's Shrine

The visit to the National Shrine of Our Lady, Knock, was always expected to be one of the highlights of the 'Pilgrimage of Grace' – and so it proved to be. From all walks of life they came, to venerate the Relics of St Thérèse of Lisieux. Thousands arrived at the famous Marian village which was *en fête* for the weekend.

A large crowd took part in the prayerful procession through the village from the Carmelite convent to the basilica. Archbishop Michael Neary was on hand to recite the opening prayers, and Mgr Dominick Grealy, Administrator of the Shrine, welcomed St Thérèse to Knock, 'a place made holy by the feet of millions'. Thérèse was only six years of age when Our Lady appeared at Knock in 1879, he said in his address of welcome.

Throughout the day, crowds continued to come and there was a constant flow through the late hours of Saturday night and into Sunday morning. The basilica was full to capacity for the Mass on Saturday afternoon. Bishop Patrick Ahern, former Auxiliary Bishop of New York and author of the best-selling book, *Maurice and Thérèse – The Story of a Love,* was the principal celebrant and preacher. He spoke of St Thérèse as a universal saint 'who speaks a message of love that is understood in every country, culture and continent.'

young people and music on organ and flute. *The White Rose,* a documentary on Thérèse, drew continual crowds throughout the visit. The next day, Fr Liam Finnerty developed the themes of mercy and love at a concelebrated Mass on the anniversary of Thérèse's offering of herself to Merciful Love. 'The visit,' one of the community remarked, 'was an unforget-table experience, bringing everyone together – local people, pilgrims and the Carmelite community – as family of God, as church.'

June 9 & 10

On Sunday the crowd swelled even more, with the arrival of the annual Down and Connor pilgrimage, led by Bishop Anthony Farquhar, chief celebrant at the afternoon Mass. The homily was once again given by Bishop Ahern, who spoke of St Thérèse and the 'Little Way': 'a way that is rooted in the gospel and to which everyone can aspire'.

'Apart from the Pope's visit in 1979, it is the biggest crowd ever seen in Knock,' Mgr Grealy remarked, 'well over 75,000 people have passed through the basilica in the last two days.' Surely a remarkable tribute to the unique place held by Knock Shrine within the hearts of the Irish people and one that reflects the universal appeal of St Thérèse herself, the Little Flower of Lisieux.

June 11-13

Joy and Jubilation!

Loughrea had never seen anything like it. Over fifty thousand people gathered into the town for a three-day festival in honour of St Thérèse. The town itself was ablaze with banners, flags, bunting and pictures of the saint, while the glorious weather added to the air of celebration. Because the town is host to both Carmelite nuns and friars and also to the cathedral of the diocese, Loughrea was especially privileged, with the Reliquary visiting three centres.

The Thérèsemobile arrived a little late because of the huge numbers waiting in the various towns and villages along the road, but it made little difference to the enthusiastic people. Led by Bishop John Kirby, the crowd – including the two Carmelite communities, hundreds of children and the local girls' school band – waited at Athenry Road to welcome the Reliquary and escort it to the Carmelite abbey. Fr Finian Monahan, OCD, Prior, welcomed everyone who had gathered for the historic event. In the afternoon there was a Healing Service with Anointing of the Sick, and that night the abbey was packed for

the concelebrated Mass, as Fr Finian spoke on the life of St Thérèse and her central insight into God's merciful love as she had discovered it in the gospel. There was veneration throughout the night, with readings, prayers and devotions.

Sr Philomena, Prioress, and the Carmelite community were at the convent door to welcome their sister, St Thérèse, when she arrived at the Convent of St Joseph on the Tuesday. There was a quiet, prayerful atmosphere throughout the day and a constant flow of people, savouring the silence and stillness of the convent chapel. Bishop Kirby spoke at the evening Mass of the significance of St Thérèse's 'Little Way' and the simplicity of her message. The chapel stayed open throughout the night. In the morning there was a special veneration service for the primary school children, before the Reliquary left for the cathedral.

Although it was only a short distance from the convent, it took an hour for the large procession to wind its way through the streets of the town to St Brendan's Cathedral. Every parish in the diocese was represented and carried a banner with the name of the parish. Bishop Kirby spoke of the impact St Thérèse's visit had already had on the town and diocese.

In the afternoon, the cathedral overflowed with people, sick and suffering, in wheel-chairs and on stretchers, all present for a Healing Service.

The cathedral was filled to capacity for the youth Mass that evening. Bishop Kirby spoke of St Thérèse as a young saint whose life was a source of inspiration and encouragement for all young people and an invitation to them to become more fully involved in the life of the church. There was a wonderful atmosphere during the midnight Mass. Fr Frank Quinn, OCD spoke movingly of St Thérèse's insight into the compassionate and tender love of God, the gentle Father revealed through the pages of the New Testament. The Mass was followed by a torchlight procession around the grounds of the cathedral. For many, this was the highlight of a remarkable three-day visit to Loughrea, beautifully coordinated, for which Fr Cathal Geraghty, Administrator, and the wonderful team of volunteers from the three venues must take the highest possible praise.

June 14

Bláithín sa Spidéal

From Loughrea, the Thérèsemobile journeyed to Cill Éinne Church, Spiddal, in the heart of the Gaeltacht. Along the way, there was a short stop at Barna church where a large crowd was waiting. In Spiddal, the entire ceremony was conducted in the Irish language, and over three thousand people, including the Bishop of Galway, James McLoughlin, were present during the four-hour stopover. An tAthair Tomás Ó Cadháin and visiting clergy received the Reliquary. The Relics were carried into the church to the haunting melody of *Gráigí Íosa,* specially composed for the occasion by Gráinne Ní Fhatharta, arranged by Charlie Lennon and sung by Mairéad Ní Fhlatharta. The visit ended with evening Mass, accompanied by Irish hymns and music sung by the local choir and the children's choir, and traditional Irish music played by Johnny Connolly, Charlie Lennon, Eilis Lennon and Mattie Joe Shéamuis. The homily was given by an tAthair Cillín Curran, OCD, a native of Spiddal, who spoke of St Thérèse as someone with 'a faithful heart', a heart that kept her close to her family and friends, and to the teaching of Jesus in the gospels.

The Relics were carried to the Thérèsemobile accompanied by the hymn, *Gráigí Íosa.* Fr Linus Ryan, National Coordinator, requested a traditional Irish tune, *Amárach lá 'le Pádraig* especially for the occasion, which was played

on the accordian by Johnny Connolly as a 'slán abhaile' to the Relics of St Thérèse.

Bhí slua mór baillithe ag Cill Éinne sa Spidéal chun ómós a thabhairt do thaisí Naomh Treasa. Bhí daoine as chuile áit i gConamara i láthair agus chan cóir Scoil Éinne ceol le haghaidh na h-ócáide. Bhí boladh rósanna in chuile áit i séipéal an Spidéil agus níor chuir an tuile báistigh taobh amuigh as do aon duine. Ní dhéanfear dearmad go deo ar theacht thaisí Naomh Treasa go Conamara.

Ní fheicimid a leithéid arís.

The Galway Festival

People were able to 'watch the sun go down on Galway Bay' as the Reliquary did not arrive at the Cathedral of Our Lady Assumed into Heaven and St Nicholas, Galway, until late evening. On the way into the city, the Reliquary made a short stop at the Poor Clare convent on Nun's Island. From there it was carried in procession by the FCA into an already packed cathedral.

Lord Mayor of Galway, Martin Quinn, and members of the Corporation turned out in ceremonial dress, together with the local clergy and Franciscan friars. The procession was led by St Patrick's Brass Band and First Communion children from Scoil an Linbh Íosa. Bishop James McLoughlin recited prayers of welcome and spoke candidly of the widespread message of love which St Thérèse's visit was proclaiming everywhere she went.

The vast cathedral, beautifully decorated with roses and ablaze with candles, made an ideal setting to accommodate the tens of thousands who came all through the night. During the Vigil, a youth choir from France sang hymns and folk songs in Thérèse's own language. At midnight, a youth group from parishes throughout the diocese expressed, in mime, music and song, their understanding of the significance of the life and spirituality of St Thérèse for young people today. They also presented books of prayers and petitions from their parishes, and took back to each parish a rose from St Thérèse.

The Healing Service on Friday morning, for the elderly and wheelchair-bound, attracted capacity crowds. Mgr Seán O'Flaherty celebrated a farewell Mass and spoke passionately of the universal appeal of St Thérèse and the simplicity of her 'Little Way'. He added that he was 'deeply touched by the great expression of faith that the occasion had inspired.'

Bridie McNeill came to venerate the Relics. 'St Thérèse is one of those saints you can really relate to and talk to; she suffered like most of us do at some stage in our lives and she suffered with great dignity. It's hard sometimes to keep believing in God when things go wrong but I try to take a leaf out of her book at times like this.'

June 15

Little Flower Blooms in Clare

The people of Clare did their county proud when they turned out in great numbers to greet the Relics of St Thérèse of Lisieux as she arrived at the Cathedral of SS Peter and Paul in Ennis. There were overcast skies and heavy showers during the morning but the rain stopped in time for the arrival. Following a procession down O'Connell Street, accompanied by a Garda escort and an FCA colour party, and with the sounds of the famous Tulla Pipe Band, the Reliquary was carried into the cathedral by members of the Civil Defence and received by Bishop Willie Walsh. Fr Tom Hogan, Administrator, welcomed all who had come for this 'unique and grace-filled visit'.

A quiet atmosphere of joy and devotion was evident in the town as people came from all over the county. They brought flowers to be blessed, and medals with which to touch the Reliquary, and they placed petitions in the boxes provided. As veneration continued throughout the day, the congregation was led

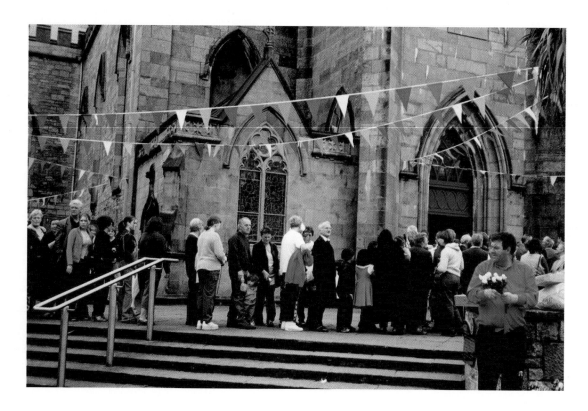

in music and prayer by school bands from the parish. The cathedral was packed for the evening Mass at which Fr Jerry Carey was the principal celebrant. Surrounding parishes came in turn to lead the prayers and singing during the Night Vigil. Fr Hogan was overjoyed at 'the great sense of cooperation inspired by the Little Flower' and he was touched by the 'great numbers reconnecting with the church'.

As the Thérèsemobile left Ennis on its way to Tallow, it made a short visit to the Poor Clare convent in St Francis Street.

Visiting priest, Fr Brendan O'Donoghue was simply overwhelmed by the incredible level of public response. 'In death, Thérèse has become much more of a missionary than she could ever have dreamt of being in life,' he said. 'There was nothing small or narrow about her prayer, it covered the whole missionary field and everywhere the gospel was preached. She never dreamt that one day she would be a missionary here in Ennis Cathedral a hundred years after her death.'

Rachel O'Connell was observing the activity around the cathedral close to midnight and decided to venture in. 'I knew there was something happening because my mother had been in earlier and she said it was very emotional. I don't know much about St Thérèse but I found it very relaxing and peaceful to be here. It's amazing to see traffic jams and queues of people at this time of night – everyone seems so happy and joyful.'

Thérèse and her Sisters

A lot of people did not realise that there were so many Carmelite convents in Ireland, and for many an added joy of the visit was to see Carmelite nuns, dressed in the brown habit of the order, standing at a church door as the Relics arrived, waiting to greet their saintly sister and taking part in the Service of Reception. Somehow it made the presence of Thérèse even more real, and highlighted the living link between the Lisieux Carmel, where Thérèse lived, and the Irish Carmels of today. For many of Thérèse's sisters in Ireland, it was an emotional homecoming, something they never thought they would see and certainly something they will never forget.

Festival of Youth

It is almost impossible to describe the atmosphere of joy and celebration that prevailed in the picturesque town of Tallow during the two-day festival in honour of St Thérèse. Most of the ceremonies took place in the open air and St Thérèse blessed the occasion with fine weather! The whole town and surrounding area seemed to be involved, as over fifty thousand people passed through the convent grounds over the weekend.

The Thérèsemobile was welcomed at Tallow Bridge by the Carmelite community together with a huge crowd – including the Cistercian nuns from nearby Glencairn Abbey and the monks from Mount Melleray – and was escorted to the convent by a Brass and Reed band and rows of dancing children. A magnificent floral tribute adorned the Tallow convent gate and the celebration began with an open-air Mass at which Bishop William Lee was the chief celebrant; the homily was given by Fr Eugene McCaffrey, OCD. From 11 o'clock on Saturday night until dawn, over two thousand young people gathered for a 'Festival of Youth' – a marvellous celebration which began with a presentation of the liturgical pageant, *Shower of Roses,* and continued throughout the night with music, song and prayers.

Youth, family and the sick were in prominent focus during the Tallow visit. On Sunday, the feast of Corpus Christi, the Anointing of the Sick in the monastery grounds was especially moving. A family Mass in the evening, at which Fr Michael Farrell, PP, was the chief celebrant, saw one of the largest congregations of the entire weekend. Monday was another day for the youth, and for many people the highlight of the visit was the closing Mass attended by two thousand school children from Tallow and west Waterford, who lined the streets of the town as the Thérèsemobile left for Limerick.

For the sisters, this had been a wonderful occasion and they were overjoyed at the response. 'One of the family coming to visit her sisters,' said Sr Patrice, who had worked so assiduously on both national and local level, to make the visit of the Relics such a huge success. 'St Thérèse has affected the lives of so many, down through the years, and her presence was felt everywhere for the weekend. People need a role model, and who better than St Thérèse, someone they can relate to?'

The visit ended with the blessing of an impressive sculpture to commemorate St Thérèse's historic visit. The people of Tallow also presented a beautiful Waterford glass bowl, carved with the words, 'Love alone counts', as a commemorative gift for the Lisieux Carmel.

Sr Anne Francis who, at twenty-three years of age, is one of the youngest members of the Tallow community, gave her reaction: 'Thérèse is a real friend to everybody and it doesn't matter who or what you are. I don't know what it is about her. I didn't know much about her until I was nineteen and then I read her autobiography. The first time I came to Tallow happened to be at the time that Thérèse was declared a Doctor of the Church and it opened up a whole new understanding of her.'

June 18

Thérèse of Limerick

'Thérèse of Limerick' was the bold heading in the *Evening Echo* on the day that St Thérèse arrived at St John's Cathedral, Limerick. Overcast skies and a light drizzle did not dampen the enthusiastic response of the huge crowds queueing ten deep outside the cathedral.

The Thérèsemobile stopped outside Limerick Prison and was escorted to the cathedral by prison officers, members of Limerick Fire Brigade and the City of Limerick Brass Band; there, it was received by Bishop Donal Murray. The ceremony was graced by the presence of the Carmelite nuns from Tallow who had travelled with the Reliquary. The cathedral was packed for the evening Mass as Bishop Murray spoke of the extraordinary influence which the life and teaching of St Thérèse had had on the whole church over the past hundred years. 'Even before she was canonised, Pope St Pius X regarded her as the greatest saint of modern times. What is so great about her is that she found her way to God in the most ordinary way.'

The cathedral remained open all night to meet the demand of the people; at times there were queues of up to three hours as people from all over the diocese came to honour St Thérèse.

Sr Noelle O'Sullivan was one of a group of pilgrims from the Holy Cross Parish in Charleville, Co Cork, and she spoke of her personal delight at being a part of this joyous occasion. 'Many of those travelling are invalids, they are suffering from different ailments, from bad hearts to broken legs,' she said. 'We knew it would be a difficult trip for some of the group, but they were determined to be here.'

Before leaving the city, the Thérèsemobile visited Limerick Prison. Like the earlier visit to Dublin's Mountjoy Prison, this brief stop proved a particularly poignant and momentous occasion, one that crossed all boundaries and extended the hand of friendship to the marginalised members of society.

Prison chaplain, Fr Pat Hogan conducted a Prayer Service at which each and every prisoner was given the opportunity to venerate the Relics. The prisoners, together with the Ballybrowne Church Choir, provided the music. Deputy Governor Walsh described the short visit as 'a tremendous occasion which will do a lot of good'.

The positive response of the Limerick people was echoed in the weekly newspaper by journalist, Patricia Feehily. 'We were all children again, touched by something very simple that we'll probably never again get a chance to experience.'

The Kerry Rose!

They came in their thousands from all over the 'Kingdom' to Killarney, the country's top tourist town, to greet a very different kind of visitor, who came not for the scenery but for the people themselves. The Thérèsemobile arrived in glorious sunshine, described as Fr Michael Fleming as 'a gift from St Thérèse'. The Reliquary was escorted to St Mary's Cathedral by a guard of honour, accompanied by the music of the Gleneagle Band and the Knights of Malta, who carried the casket into the sanctuary.

Bishop Bill Murphy was there to receive the Reliquary and expressed the hope that the visit would be 'a time of great grace and blessing for the town and the diocese'. 'We have been waiting a long time for this day and now at last it is here,' he said. 'I welcome St Thérèse, not her Relics or her bones, but the saint herself.'

Outside, an almost carnival atmosphere existed as the cathedral grounds were filled with waiting people and stalls selling souvenirs and memorabilia. Over thirty priests, joined by visiting Bishop Joseph Sartoris of Los

June 19

Angeles, concelebrated the evening Mass with Bishop Murphy who told the congregation that Thérèse had been 'a liberating force in the church', and 'had restored the true image of God as revealed in the gospels'. There was a constant stream of people as the cathedral remained open all night, and each

of the ten deaneries in the diocese was assigned a specific time to visit. Once again, the people packed the cathedral for the early morning Mass. The Relics left at midday for Cork, after a short Farewell Service.

If there is one person who deserved a front row seat in St Mary's Cathedral, Killarney, it is Patricia Lyne, whose family devotion to St Thérèse speaks for itself. 'My mother,' she said, 'always read passages from her book. In the early fifties, my father and uncle travelled to Lisieux where they met St Thérèse's sister, Céline. They spoke with her and my father told her of the family devotion, while my uncle, who was a canon in Bristol at the time, told her that he was building a church at Filton in Bristol. It was opened in 1960 and dedicated to St Thérèse.'

But that's not where this story ends. Patricia, one of a family of twelve, was blessed with a deep affection for the Little Flower which spans three generations. Four of her sisters were named after members of the Martin family – Thérèse, Pauline, Céline and Léonie – while her nephew is Martin Louis and her niece Zélie, after Thérèse's own parents. Not surprisingly, Patricia herself is thrilled to be able to celebrate today in her own home town. 'We just relate to her way of life and that's why the whole family are coming here today. It is incredible.'

June 20

A Rose by the Lee

The people of Cork had to wait ten weeks for the visit of St Thérèse, but for the twelve thousand who had gathered outside the 'North Cathedral', it was well worth the wait. A colour party of boy scouts, girl guides and lines of school children formed a guard of honour, and the music of the Butter Exchange Band echoed around the cathedral grounds as Bishop John Buckley received the Reliquary.

This was a day for the children, who were very much to the fore in an extremely moving Ceremony of Welcome directed by the coordinator of the Cork visit, Frances Feehely. The solo voice of a young girl sang the haunting melody, *Miracles*, as the Relics entered the hushed Cathedral of St Mary and St Anne. Then three boys placed rose bushes – to be planted later in the cathedral grounds – beside the casket. There followed a graceful liturgical dance, to the music of one of St Thérèse's best-known poems, *A Rose Unpetalled*. Finally, Thérèse was given a real Cork 'Céad Míle Fáilte' in a delightful Irish dance sequence.

To commemorate the visit, the Organising Committee issued a beautiful colour brochure entitled, *I will Spend my Heaven doing Good on Earth*, with photographs of Thérèse, quotations from her writings and background information on the saint.

Veneration continued throughout the day and the crowds grew larger as night approached. It is estimated that over eighty thousand people visited the cathedral during the twenty-two hours. Spokesperson for the Cork diocese, Fr Tom Hayes was not surprised at the interest in the Relics of the Little Flower. 'Thérèse has been in the popular consciousness of the Irish people long before now,' he said. 'The story of her life is very close to the lives of many people today.'

Before leaving the city, there was a detour to Cork Prison, where veneration took place for a short period. This visit was at the request of the Governor, Frank McCarthy, and the prison authorities. 'Unlike everyone else, the prisoners do not have the freedom to come and venerate the Relics,' said Bishop Buckley. 'I think St Thérèse herself would be very pleased with the visit.' After a brief stopover at the prison, there was another short, private visit to the Poor Clare convent in College Road.

Philomena Ahern was also there. 'I came with my sister. I have been living in England for the past twenty years but have never seen a tour like this. I came over especially because I still have a copy of a prayer to St Thérèse that I had on my wedding day. We brought roses to be blessed and are bringing them later today to our parents' grave. I think they would have liked to be here, so we're thinking of them today.'

Midsummer Festival

On a glorious midsummer day, Cobh was *en fête* for the visit of St Thérèse to St Colman's Cathedral. The magnificent cathedral was an ideal setting for such a memorable occasion. Members of the Cobh Urban Council, together with the ex-servicemen and women of the army and navy and the local Confraternity Band, accompanied the Thérèsemobile from the town centre. The rich peals of the 47-stroke bell carillon – the largest in Ireland – echoed across the harbour, as marines from nearby Haulbowline Station carried the Reliquary into the cathedral. Bishop John Magee said the opening prayer and welcomed all who had come to Cobh for this historic occasion. The pupils from Cobh Vocational School and Scoil Coláiste Muire led the congregation in the readings and prayers. The cathedral itself was festooned with pictures of St Thérèse and quotations from her writings. As well as confessors, spiritual counsellors were also available throughout the day to offer help, support and guidance.

At the evening Mass, Bishop Magee, speaking with obvious affection for the Little Flower, referred to her discovery of her vocation to be 'love in the heart of the church'. Her visit to Cobh, he added, was an invitation to base our own lives on the only reality that really matters: God's unconditional and unchanging love for us. A special feature of the Cobh visit was the continuous relay of choirs who sang during the visit. At midnight, local curate, Fr Timothy Fouhy, and the youth choir led reflections and meditations which added to the prayerful atmosphere in the cathedral. The Thérèsemobile left Cobh at midday and made a short visit to the Benedictine nuns in the town, giving the cloistered community an opportunity to venerate the Relics and also to invite the small group of visitors to see the beautiful biblical garden attached to the convent.

Sinéad McGowan, home on holiday from New York, was in Cobh. 'It's an incredible feeling being here, especially at night. There's such a peaceful and intimate atmosphere. Back home, you don't really know anyone in the church; here it's more immediate and personable. I hardly know anything about St Thérèse but I'm curious about her now.'

June 22

On Home Ground

'This is the day the Lord has made, let us rejoice and be glad' was how Bishop John Magee welcomed the Relics of St Thérèse to the Carmelite community at Castlemartyr. 'St Thérèse has come home,' he added, 'to her own brothers and to the college named after her.' It was indeed a sort of homecoming ceremony as Fr Pat Beecher and the Carmelite community met the Thérèsemobile at the college gates and escorted it along the avenue, lined with school children holding flowers. The Castlemartyr Youth Choir led the way as soldiers from Collins Barracks carried the Reliquary into the oratory.

The spacious college grounds afforded ample parking space for the thousands of people who visited the Relics over a twenty-two-hour period. The beautiful college oratory, adorned with bouquets of flowers, made a perfect setting for the Reliquary. Because of the glorious weather, it was possible to hold many of the ceremonies in the open air. In

the evening, over six thousand people spread across the lawns around the statue of St Thérèse, for a concelebrated Mass sung by the parish choir of St Joseph's, Castlemartyr. 'I doubt if this historic place, with its ancient castle and Georgian mansion, has ever seen such a sight,' said Fr Peter Cryan, OCD in his homily. 'On this day, the feast of the Sacred Heart, in the college that bears her name, it is only right to remind ourselves of St Thérèse's message: that love alone counts.'

Throughout the visit, many people enjoyed the video on the life of St Thérèse, which was shown continuously, and also the exhibition

June 22

on her life and teaching. Over two thousand people attended the early morning Mass at which Fr Jim Noonan, OCD, a native of Cork and missionary from Nigeria, spoke of Thérèse as 'the greatest missionary of all, even though she never left her convent.'

As the Thérèsemobile headed for the SMA church in Blackrock, it made a brief stopover *en route* at St Mary's Parish Church, Carrigtwohill.

Twenty-three-year-old Patrick McCabe came with his mother, Peggy, at 2 o'clock in the morning. 'My mother told me a lot about St Thérèse over the years and we always went to the Triduum in our village. I'm amazed at the crowds. I didn't realise she was so young when she died.'

'St Thérèse never lets you down,' added his mother. 'I've prayed to her for so many things – my family, my friends and my health – and she always comes up trumps. I would not have missed this for anything and wanted to come at night when it is more special.'

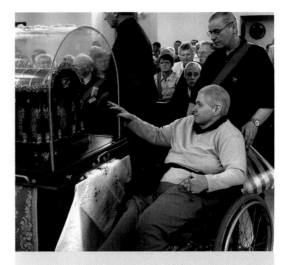

A Gospel Scene

Scenes straight out of the New Testament were repeated in many places as the Thérèsemobile travelled throughout the country. Patients from local hospitals, convalescent homes and nursing homes were brought in wheelchairs or carried on stretchers and placed near the side of the road as the Reliquary passed by. 'I have never seen anything like it,' said Pat Sweeney, manager of the Thérèsemobile, 'The faith and joy of both the patients and staff is something I will never forget.' He added: 'We were only too pleased to stop and pray with them. Faith like this can move mountains.'

Patroness of the Missions

Blackrock, Cork, is well-known for its missionary communities: the Franciscan Missionary Sisters, the OLA Sisters, Ardfoyle, the Ursuline Sisters and the SMA community are all located in this area. Therefore, it was natural that the visit of St Thérèse to Blackrock Road would have a special missionary focus.

A large crowd was waiting at Ashton School to escort the Reliquary to the SMA church when the Thérèsemobile arrived. A colour party of scouts and young children, accompanied by a lone piper, led the way. The streets were colourful with banners, flags and bunting and the church itself was beautifully decorated and illuminated for the occasion. The people of Blackrock had prepared, over the three days leading to the visit of St Thérèse, with a Triduum preached by Fr Philip Brennan, O Carm. The Relics were received by Provincial, Fr John Quinlan, SMA, Bishop Patrick Harrington, SMA from Lodwar, Kenya, and the SMA community. During the Opening Ceremony, precedence was given to physically disabled people and senior citizens, assisted by the Order of Malta, St John's Ambulance and members of the Civil Defence. Fr John Quinlan was the chief celebrant at the evening Mass; he spoke about St Thérèse as Patroness of the Missions, and of the impact of her spirituality on the work of the SMA missions over the years. He talked about the beautiful shrine of St Thérèse, erected in the church in 1929, just four years after her canonisation. This shrine is the focus of the annual novena – the largest in the city – which has taken place in Blackrock Road ever since the shrine was built. Every year on the feast of St Thérèse, SMA missionaries were commissioned prior to their assignment overseas. In all, over seven hundred SMA missionaries were commissioned in front of St Thérèse's shrine.

A crowd of over twenty thousand people visited the Reliquary, and many remarked on the prayerful silence and the atmosphere of reverence that prevailed.

June 24

At the Centre of the World

Kinsale was the last Carmelite house to receive the Relics of St Thérèse, and it was indeed an occasion of great joy and celebration for the people of the town. On a beautiful Sunday afternoon the Prior, Fr Michael Morrissey, O Carm and the Carmelite community met the Thérèsemobile; they were joined by members of the Carmelite Secular Order, First Communion children and representatives of the UDC. The afternoon was graced by the presence of His Excellency Patrick Coveney, Papal Nuncio to New Zealand, who is a native of Kinsale, as well as by the presence of the Rector of St Multose's Church, Canon David Williams, and the retired rector, Canon David Peare.

Fr Morrissey said that the people of Kinsale had been waiting a long time for the visit of St Thérèse but that it was well worth the wait. 'This is our day,' he said. 'For us today, Kinsale is at the centre of the world.' Fr Jimmy Murray, O Carm also spoke of the visit of St Thérèse as an invitation to follow her along the way of love and to move closer to God and to each other in friendship and prayer. A lovely feature of the Opening Ceremony was the precedence given to senior citizens, the sick and infirm, and after they had venerated the Relics they received a special blessing and anointing. Another feature of the Kinsale visit was the continuous convoy of coaches that came from all parts of west Cork. The crowds grew larger as the day progressed and veneration continued throughout the night in an atmosphere of reverence and prayerfulness.

Sixteen-year-old Claire Short was in Kinsale. 'I've been very sick for the past few months. I've been in hospital and missed a lot of school. I've lost contact with a lot of my friends. When you're sick, you really need to believe in something, and when I go back to hospital I'll read Thérèse's book because I've heard so much about her. I'd like to know her better.'

June 25

A Star Attraction

Thurles is well used to hosting big events, such as Munster Finals, Fleadhanna and Féilte, but had never seen anything like this before. It is estimated that over 75,000 people flocked to the town during the visit of St Thérèse, travelling from all over the Archdiocese of Cashel and Emly.

A large crowd was waiting for the Thérèse-mobile when it arrived in Liberty Square on an afternoon of glorious sunshine. From there, the Reliquary, led by piper, Philip Egan, was escorted to the Cathedral of the Assumption by the Administrator, Fr Eugene Everard, members of the Children of Mary and junior boys from Scoil Ailbe, carrying roses. It was received at the cathedral steps by Archbishop Dermot Clifford and carried into the sanctuary by the Order of Malta. First Communion children from the Presentation, Ursuline, Gaelscoil and CBS schools formed a guard of honour. In his words of welcome, Archbishop Clifford said that it was wonderful that a saint could cause such a sense of excitement and bring together the whole town and archdiocese in a celebration of joy and unity. 'Today, Thérèse is our Star Attraction,' he said. 'In St Thérèse's own words: everything is a grace.' He continued: 'Certainly, for us today, it is a grace to have in our presence the greatest saint of modern times.'

June 25

Such were the numbers of people attending the evening Mass, celebrated by Archbishop Clifford, that the crowds overflowed into the cathedral grounds and along the streets. In his opening address, the archbishop said, 'The reason for the popularity of this young saint is surely the love radiating from her heart. Her "Little Way" could be subtitled "holiness made simple". She reminds us that all the Lord really wants is our feeble efforts given out of love.' In the homily, Fr Eugene McCaffrey, OCD said that the secret of St Thérèse was that she rediscovered the true heart of God as revealed in the gospel.

Veneration continued non-stop throughout the night. It was incredible to see the throng of people queueing on both sides of the cathedral in the small hours of the morning, waiting patiently for their turn to visit the Reliquary. The cathedral's choir and folk group, together with Bóthar na Naomh Choir, added to the prayerfulness of the visit.

After Mass on Tuesday morning, the Relics left for the next stage of the journey to Waterford, waved and applauded by a large crowd of people.

Love Alone Counts

It was a nice coincidence that the Relics of St Thérèse arrived at Holy Trinity Cathedral, Waterford, on 26 June to visit the last of the 26 diocesan cathedrals in Ireland. Before the Relics arrived, a wonderful atmosphere had been generated as the congregation joined in prayer, singing and reflection. The cathedral itself was beautifully decorated, and there were two huge photographs of St Thérèse in the sanctuary. Excerpts from her writings were displayed throughout the cathedral, together with background information on her life and message.

Bishop of Waterford and Lismore, William Lee, joined by Carmelite nuns from the diocese, was on hand to meet the Relics at the cathedral door. The bishop recited prayers of welcome and the casket was carried inside by members of the Defence Forces. 'We give thanks for this moment of grace,' Bishop Lee said. 'The Little Flower has taken Ireland by storm, but we should remember that her Relics point to her person, and to her deep and abiding love for God. Her message is very simple: love alone counts.'

To facilitate veneration, Masses were held in the nearby St Patrick's Church. In the cathedral itself, people were able to attend Morning and Evening Prayer and a special dawn Mass on Wednesday. Waterford Cathedral's Administrator, Fr Willie Ryan, estimated that up to forty thousand came to venerate the Relics.

After leaving the cathedral at noon on Wednesday, the Reliquary made a brief stop at St Patrick's Hospital, to the joy of the many patients who were waiting for this very special moment. The Thérèsemobile then made its way to the nearby sports ground where a helicopter was waiting to convey the Reliquary to Lough Derg.

Hannah Mai Hutchinson from Ballydavid was in Waterford for her third all-night Vigil. When the Relics were in Killarney, she spent her first full night of Vigil in the cathedral. Two days later, she was in Cobh for another all-night Vigil and then made her way to Waterford to spend the night, once again, in the presence of the Relics and to say goodbye as Thérèse left Waterford the next day. There is no doubt that Hannah Mai represents countless people whose spirit of prayer and devotion accompanied Thérèse everywhere she went.

June 27

An Island Pilgrim

St Patrick's Purgatory, Lough Derg, was meant to be the last stop on the original seventy-four-day 'Pilgrimage of Grace'. Instead, it became the first, in a number of ways: the first time St Thérèse had travelled by helicopter in Ireland, and the first time a helicopter had ever landed on Lough Derg. There was a wonderful air of excitement and anticipation as the helicopter approached Lough Derg and circled the island before landing. Fr Eugene McCaffrey, OCD travelled on the helicopter from Waterford. 'It was marvellous to see the pilgrims gathered in front of the basilica,' he said, 'waving, cheering and clapping as the helicopter touched down.' The Reliquary was received by Mgr Richard Mohan, Prior, and carried into the basilica by six barefoot pilgrims as the whole congregation joined in the singing of the Lourdes *Magnificat*. The Relics were then placed in front of the statue of St Thérèse, one of only two in the basilica. The opening prayers included the recitation of the Litany of St Thérèse. 'This is indeed the day the Lord has

'made,' Fr Richard said, echoing the words of the entrance hymn. 'For us,' he continued, 'it is the fulfilment of a dream, a dream that one day St Thérèse would come, as St Patrick did, on pilgrimage to Lough Derg.' It seemed fitting for St Thérèse to visit Lough Derg, a sanctuary hallowed by hundreds of years of prayer and penance and steeped in Celtic tradition and history – a natural marriage of early Christianity and the spirituality of the twenty-first century.

Barefoot pilgrims continued to visit the Reliquary during the afternoon, in between the traditional rounds of 'doing the beds' and telling the beads. The light drizzle did not lessen the joy for the thousand or so pilgrims who had the luxury of spending as much time as they wanted close to the casket. Fr La Flynn was the principal celebrant at the evening Mass. 'St Thérèse,' he said, 'is the little child in the gospel whom Jesus placed before his disciples. We are all called to the same childlike trust and confidence exemplified in her life.'

At dusk, the pilgrims gathered in front of the basilica to say goodbye to St Thérèse. It was with sad and lonely hearts that they watched the helicopter lift off across the lake into the fading light. It landed at Gormanston Army Camp where there was a short service led by chaplain, Fr Robert McCabe for the soldiers and their families. The Reliquary then moved on, towards Wexford Park.

July 1

Up, Up and Away!

After Lough Derg, the Thérèsemobile slowly made its way from Gormanston Camp to Wexford, staying for an all-night Vigil at the Visitation monastery, Stamullen. There is a strong link between Thérèse's family and the Visitation Order. Her sister, Léonie, was a member of the Order at Caen, and her Aunt Marie-Louise belonged to the Visitation convent at Le Mans, where the two eldest Martin girls, Marie and Pauline, had been educated. As the Thérèsemobile passed through Dublin, it called at Nazareth House, Malahide Road, before moving on to the Cistercian abbey in Roscrea, for an all-night Vigil. From there, a visit was made to Abbeyleix parish church and St Dympna's Hospital, Carlow. The last official call was, as Thérèse would have wished, a visit to the sick at St Brigid's Hospice in the Curragh.

On Sunday, 1 July, a Thanksgiving Celebration took place in Wexford Park, attended by the Papal Nuncio, Most Rev Giuseppe Lazzarotto, and hosted by Bishop Brendan Comiskey and the Diocese of Ferns. In glorious sunshine, fifteen thousand people

enjoyed a feast of music, song, mime and dance. 'St Thérèse's visit has been subversive,' Bishop Brendan announced, 'for all who peddle a false God, a God not of the gospels with their simple, yet powerful, message of love, mercy and forgiveness.'

Children brought five thousand balloons into the stadium and these were released, carrying a message of peace to the country and to the world as the massed voices rang out in the clear summer air: 'Let there be peace.'

The atmosphere was electric as the Reliquary was carried to the waiting helicopter and lifted off into the sky to cheers and waves while the crowds sang, *Now is the hour when we must say goodbye.* It was like saying goodbye to one of the family, and for all the joy and wonderful memories of St Thérèse's visit to Ireland, there were tears and an understandable sadness as the helicopter flew out of sight on the start of the return journey to Lisieux.

It was hard to believe that our 'Pilgrimage of Grace' was now over. Eleven weeks – eighty-eight days – on the road: twelve thousand miles of travel; seventy-five official venues and many more unofficial ones in roadside stops, detours and diversions. It is estimated that three million people came to venerate the Relics. It is obvious that something far greater than the bones of a dead saint was involved. St Thérèse has struck a chord in the hearts of the Irish people, and the example of her life and her 'Little Way' of confidence and trust has rekindled a spark of love, hidden in many hearts, waiting to be set free. 'A single spark of love,' she once remarked, 'can set the whole world on fire.' May that fire of love, rekindled by this 'Pilgrimage of Grace', continue to burn brightly in our hearts.

'The Story of a Love'

If there is one subject Bishop Patrick Ahern of New York is passionate about, it is his relationship with St Thérèse and his extraordinary devotion to her, which has developed and matured through the years.

'From the first moment I read her autobiography, I thought, "This is the person for me, and this is the saint for me." She spoke to me in every line of her book; she knew what I needed to hear and I was hooked; and throughout my whole life I have never been unhooked. Never have I lost the fundamental conviction that this woman is unique and, in my opinion, simply the greatest Christian figure since Jesus. I know that may sound fanatical but it's not just my own opinion, it's that of many scholars and writers.'

Bishop Ahern fervently believes that the essence of Thérèse's greatness lies in her humanity, and the thing that makes her so human and so real is the way in which she dealt with pain and suffering. 'She was a very tense teenager, hypersensitive, and she suffered greatly all through her life,' he said. 'Today we are living in a world of pain and she can identify with the trials of modern life.'

Bishop Ahern's own relationship with Thérèse is a very palpable and personal one. 'I rely on her very heavily and ask her help. She never lets me down; she has never made me feel bad about myself, no matter what I have done. She bolsters my self-esteem and encourages me to keep going. Thérèse is unique. She is "the greatest saint of modern times' and if I could equal her, there would be two of us!'

'A Rose that never Dies'

In the end, it was not about Relics, not even the Relics of a great saint. It was about people. What happened in Ireland, from Easter Sunday till 1 July, 2001, was essentially a People's Movement, at its very best. People came because they wanted to come; they came spontaneously and joyfully. A parish priest in the west of Ireland caught the mood perfectly, as he saw the crowds streaming towards the church: 'People know where the clover is,' he said. And it was for this they came: the clover of the gospel. They knew they were welcome, at home with one of themselves. Thérèse of Lisieux revealed herself as everybody's saint, a universal sister, alive in the hearts of countless thousands of people. They did not come for lengthy sermons or long liturgies; they came to pray, to touch, to be close to someone they knew could read their hearts and who radiated a simple message of love. In the end, people place the highest value on holiness, and when they recognise it they want to be near it. Her visit was a social as well as a religious event. One of the extraordinary things about the visit was how whole communities and parishes bonded together, as doors and hearts were thrown open. Her presence created community, prayerfulness, and an atmosphere of support and understanding. Everywhere, there were smiles, tears of joy and a deepen-ing of friendships. Thérèse touched the heart of the nation in a way no other religious event ever did, and she did so at a local level – along the roadway, in the streets and in the towns. She was accessible day and night, a friend among friends.

The visit of St Thérèse to Ireland, like her life, defies logic and reason, cause and effect, and the self-serving edicts of a consumer society. It released a deep spirituality in the Irish people and highlighted the need in the church for a spirituality of popular devotion. Thérèse not only spoke of love, she also showed a 'way' to live it simply and humbly. She brought holiness into the streets, the homes and the workplace. Her visit gave new hope to thousands of people and renewed all who came with the true spirit of the gospel.

Perhaps, even after the extraordinary events of Summer 2001, we are still no closer to understanding the mystery of her appeal. Yet her appeal cannot be ignored and, as far as we can see, will continue well into this century, as she continues her journey of love throughout all continents. Her dream is becoming a reality: 'to preach the gospel to the four corners of the world'. Brendan Kennelly beautifully catches the wonder of it all in the closing line of his poem on St Thérèse:

Withering, she grows, a rose that never dies.